LOTTERY-WINNERS' GUIDE

When it Happens to You

SHAYNE JONES

Cover by Stonepatch Design

Set in Times New Roman

Printed in the United States of America

ISBN 0-9768673-7-0

Footpath Publishing
Post Office Box 724088
Atlanta, Georgia 31139
www.footpathpublishing.com

Table of Contents

Sales Department

Shipping Department

3 Psychology Department

4 Planning Department

Transportation Department

5 Claims Department

6 Finance Department

7 Tax Department

Accounts Payable Department

8 Public Relations Department

9 Privacy Department

Security Department

10 Human Resource Department

Disclaimer

This publication was conceived through the collection of valid data, thorough research and interviews. The information, recommendations and tips found within this reading should be used only as an educational awareness tool and not as precise instruction. As a general compilation, this guidebook does not intend to describe the rules, regulations, or policies of any specific state, province, lottery agency or game. Further, this book is not affiliated with any lottery game, game-of-chance, lottery agency or government entity.

While various organizations are referenced within this reading, no validation or certification is suggested or implied as to the information provided by said organizations. No expressed or implied relationship or approval of services with respect to any referenced organization is made. This book does not advertise, in whole or in part, any lottery game or game-of-chance.

It is recognized that state policies and lottery regulations vary and that this work attempts only to reveal the similarities of lottery game rules, processes and winning procedures. And despite everyone's best efforts, the constantly changing nature of policies, regulations and procedures makes it impossible to guarantee absolute accuracy.

This publication is sold with the understanding that the author or anyone involved in its creation, distribution or sales is not engaged in rendering legal, accounting or other professional services and advice. This disclaimer applies to both isolated and aggregate uses of the information.

In order to confirm the legality and/or authenticity of any information in this guide, all lottery-jackpot winners should consult licensed professionals in the state where the ticket was purchased as well the state in which they hold residence. As the author's bestseller, this book is believed to be newsworthy, important to the development of lottery players and entertaining.

Statistical Methodology

Originally included in this reading was a statistical methodology review, which analyzes the accuracy of data and findings in Chapter

One's Mythology Department. Due to the length and complexity, the methodology appendix was not included in this edition.

The review not only examines the statistical methods used in collecting and analyzing the data, but it also scrutinizes the measures taken to ensure unbiased, reliable and valid conclusions. With high confidence levels and normal margins of error, the statistical methodologies used in these studies meet and/or exceed professional standards.

To obtain a copy of this review, please send a written request to Footpath Publishing at the address found on the copyright page in the front of the book. Please include the email address where you would like to receive the appendix. Thank you.

Problem Gambling

"Know when to say when"

Throughout the United States, governments and social organizations are available to help pathological gamblers combat addictive behavior. Not unlike abusers of drugs and alcohol, compulsive gamblers are believed to have an illness that is treatable through counseling, support groups and various other programs.

In a sense, state-run lotteries actually benefit the compulsive gambler by providing games that are not befitting to their desires, but promote responsible play and contribute resources to help-programs for all problem gamblers. A percentage of lottery ticket sales go to social programs, treatment centers, and/or hotlines that help casino, sports, lottery and bingo addicts throughout the country.

Lotteries and Gambling Problems

Critics of the legalized gambling community argue that lotteries create problem gamblers. However, this couldn't be further from the truth. While a small percentage (2%) of problem gamblers do prefer lottery games, the fact is that this method of gambling ranks at the bottom for games-of-choice. This is because lotteries do not provide the same kind of reward or enticement that interests the typical compulsive gambler.

For instance, pathological gamblers usually prefer games that provide immediate feedback. But since lottery players have to wait anywhere from 1 to 7 days to get drawing results, the lottery form of gambling is less desirable.

Instead of lottery games that require no talent or skill, the games found in casinos appeal more to heavy gamblers because skill, strategy, and proficiency in a specific game can be used to increase their odds. Only luck from the process of random selection is necessary to win a lottery.

Problem Gambling Definition

A compulsive gambler is someone whose addiction to gambling causes him or her problems in personal or professional relationships, with mental health, or with financial stability. The typical nature of a compulsive gambler is characterized by an obsession with gambling, a need for the "action" and excitement, an ever-increasing tolerance for risk, and the inability to stop gambling at any time.

If you or someone you know answers "Yes" to any of these questions, there is a good chance that either you or they have a gambling problem.

1. Have you ever gambled longer than you had planned?
2. Do you often gamble until your last dollar is gone?
3. Have thoughts of gambling caused you to lose sleep?
4. Have you used your income or savings to gamble while letting bills go unpaid?
5. Have you ever made repeated, unsuccessful attempts to stop gambling?
6. Have you broken the law or considered breaking the law to finance your gambling?
7. Have you borrowed money to finance your gambling?
8. Have you been remorseful after gambling?

9. Have you felt depressed or suicidal because of your gambling losses?
10. Have you gambled to get money to meet your financial obligations?[1]

By simply calling the toll free and confidential National Problem Gambling Helpline Network (800-522-4700), you can speak with a gambling counselor.

Admit Your Problem and Get Help

Just as with any psychological illness, the compulsive gambler needs to admit his/her problem and commit to rehabilitation. Help comes in a variety of forms, but rehabilitation starts with accepting that you have a problem and asking for help.

Regardless of your game-of-choice, lottery agencies, social organizations and support groups will assist you in getting help with your gambling addiction. If you think you have a gambling problem, don't be afraid to ask for help.

- **National Council on Problem Gambling, Inc.**
  24-Hour Crisis Intervention and Referrals
  Helpline: (800) 522-4700
  www.ncpgambling.org [2]

- **Gamblers Anonymous**
  International Service Office
  Post Office Box 17173
  Los Angeles, CA 90017
  (213) 386-8789
  www.gamblersanonymous.org [3]

Play Responsibly or Don't Play at All

Introduction

Congratulations! You have either just won the lottery or you are planning to do so in the future. Either way, you should know what lies ahead for you as a ***lottery winner***. It is not enough to be able to answer the most frequently asked questions. You must know what **to do** and what **not to do** when you hit a multimillion-dollar jackpot. If you have ever asked yourself, "What will I do when I win the lottery?" - this book is for you.

Structured like a business (because that's what managing large sums of money becomes), this guide leads you through department by department, from "Mythology" through "Claims", "Public Relations" and even "Human Resources." You will develop a clear idea of what faces you, and you will have the answers BEFORE you are tested. The targeted chapters and departments are carefully designed to guide you step by step through the maze of traps that you will surely face.

When Jack Whittaker, an accomplished businessman from West Virginia, won the POWERBALL® lottery in December 2002, even he was unsure of how to manage the largest single jackpot in history. And just as Whittaker, the owner of a successful construction company, was aware of the financial sacrifice in accepting the lump-sum payment of $170.5 million instead of the 30-year annuity of $314.9 million, it is vital to recognize that even lottery winners with proven business skills often become overwhelmed with the complexity of their decisions.

With the multitude of personal preference choices, laws, policies, security and financial management issues to be considered, it is crucial for the winner of a lottery jackpot, be it $200 or $20 million, to have good information to make smart choices. You will be called upon to make decisions about the claims process, interviews, personal privacy, helping family, friends and charities, and numerous financial management issues. At the same time, you must be prepared to make decisions about organizational beggars, industry rogues and unqualified 'professionals' who will undoubtedly come knocking at your door.

There are a sufficient number of documented cases where lottery winners abandoned caution and for one reason or another, made catastrophic errors that jeopardized their winnings. Should you, the lottery winner, react erroneously, say the wrong thing, or fail to employ the right people, you could easily find yourself on the brink of financial disaster.

But while the only way to completely avoid these decisions is not to play large jackpot lottery games, a better way is to have the information and knowledge necessary to manage such a windfall.

When we participate in lottery games, no matter how serious or casual our level of play, the possibility of a great financial windfall can make our minds work at warp speed. At first, you might think, "I would buy a new house, make a donation to the Lily Dale Church and then take my entire family and all my friends to Myrtle Beach." We all play the "what if" game, to include carefully scripted scenes where you tell your boss to "Shove it. I ain't workin' here no more!" You envision a life of luxury, your newfound wealth lasting well past your death, leaving a legacy of the good life for children and heirs. Unfortunately, the old saying "easy come, easy go" lurks behind every hastily made, uninformed decision you might make.

While these daydreams are what makes playing lottery games fun, they are also our subconscious way of preparing for the actuality of success. When you begin to analyze these intimidating questions, the technical nature of your concerns can almost be overwhelming. Some of the daunting questions we ask include:

- What would I do if I won the lottery?
- How would I react?
- How could I be so lucky?
- Would my good fortune bring me happiness or sorrow?
- What would I do first and whom could I tell?
- Could I maintain a private and secure lifestyle?
- Would I be legally obligated to share my winnings with an ex-spouse?
- I'm in this country illegally. Can I keep the money?
- Who could I trust to place, protect and invest my money?
- Would I need my attorney or accountant present when I received my winnings?
- Should I take the annuity or cash option?
- Is there any way I can legally avoid paying taxes?
- How much will I have to pay in federal, state and local taxes?
- What do I need to know about giving to family, friends and charities?
- How could I prevent financial investors from taking advantage of me?
- Would I be bankrupt in five years?

- What charities would I give to?
- If interviewed by the media, what would I say?

This book answers all of those questions, and many more. Sudden wealth will throw you curve balls you didn't even know existed. According to Joan Difuria, San Francisco psychologist, "When people don't expect it and haven't planned for it, they aren't ready for the bombardment of [decisions] and people…."[4]

While other lottery books cover magical winning strategies, this consumer guide provides the reader with relevant information about lottery games, the winning process, the experiences of other lottery-winners, a general understanding of the psychological and personal impact of "hitting a jackpot", financial management issues and an assortment of best practices and tips to help the lottery winner with their prize-winning.

In preparing for your success, don't forget the clichés that declare the person with $40 million to be no less happy than the person with $30 million and that the only thing more important than having a little money, is having a lot. Aristotle said, "…a large sum of money is simply a guarantee that we may purchase what we want in the future. Though we need nothing at the moment, it ensures the possibility of satisfying a new desire when it arises." – Good Luck!

1 Mythology Department

There are not many subjects that lend themselves to fallacy and superstition as a fantastic happenstance such as winning a ton of money in a lottery! The myths and fables abound, but it's facts you need, so let's put to rest some of the most well known myths that are floating around out there.

MYTH 1

You Will Be Struck by Lightning Before You Win a Lottery Jackpot

This myth was mathematically debunked by Dr. Ed Stanek (doctorate in physics), CEO, Iowa Lottery Commissioner. The fact is that you are far more likely to win a lottery jackpot than to be struck by lightning. Statistics gathered by the National Association of State and Provincial Lotteries (NASPL) expose the truth behind this myth.[5]

Fact: In 1996 only 91 people were killed by lightning in the United States of America.[6]

Fact: 1,136 people won $1,000,000 or more playing North American lotteries in 1996.

According to National Weather Service statistics, the average number of lightning fatalities in the U.S. each year is 67. This is considerably lower than the 1940's average of over 300 deaths per year.[7]

But while lightning fatalities continue to decline, the number of people who win lottery jackpots continues to rise. Updated records show that nearly 2000 people become millionaires each year by winning lotteries.

And unless you consider the approximate 900

people who are injured from lightning strikes each year without being killed, there is no second prize in a lightning strike. In a lottery, you win lesser amounts of money by matching only a fraction of the set of winning numbers.

FIGURE 1.1

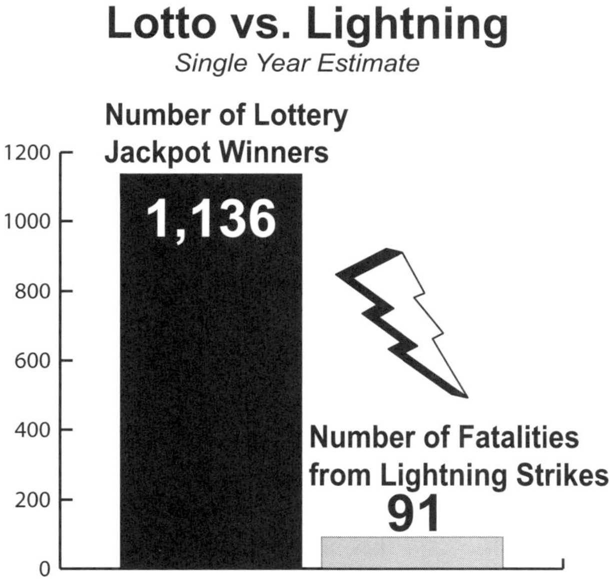

In many games, odds of 1 in 5 or 1 in 4 are not uncommon. In 1996 alone, the NASPL found that an additional 4,520 people won $100,000 or more in lotteries. Lotteries award over $50 million in prizes every day. Lightning isn't nearly that fruitful.[8]

MYTH 2

Special Numbers Win more than QUICK PICKS®

Whether you use special self-picked or computer generated quick-and-easy pick number sets, you have exactly the same statistical probability of winning a lottery jackpot. Perhaps because of purchasing habits, player preferences, or just the simplicity of buying quick-and-easy picks at the checkout counter, the majority of lottery jackpots are won with computer generated number sets.

Fact: 29% of Lottery Winners win by self-picking special numbers.

Fact: 71% of Lottery Winners win by playing quick-and-easy-pick numbers.

The people who win by using the numbers of favorite baseball players or those found in a fortune cookie are coincidental and do not win as often as QUICK PICK® players. One theoretical problem with "special numbers" is that they are commonly based on dates, magical systems or favorite numbers that, believe it or not, are likely to be used by others too.

For instance, number sets that include the dates of family members' birthdays include numbers below 31. Because this system reduces the number of possible outcomes, while at the same time increasing the likelihood of other players using the same set of digits, there is less chance for *individual* success.

You may have also heard of magical or other systems used to select "special numbers" that are suppose to increase your odds of winning. Some of these systems include frequency charts, wheeling systems and specialty computer programs. Keep in mind that such gimmicks are most often sold for profit, devoid of scientific merit, and a waste of money. A better way to increase your odds of winning a lottery is to take the money you would have spent on the miracle method and buy more tickets.

FIGURE 1.2

Winning Number Selection Rates

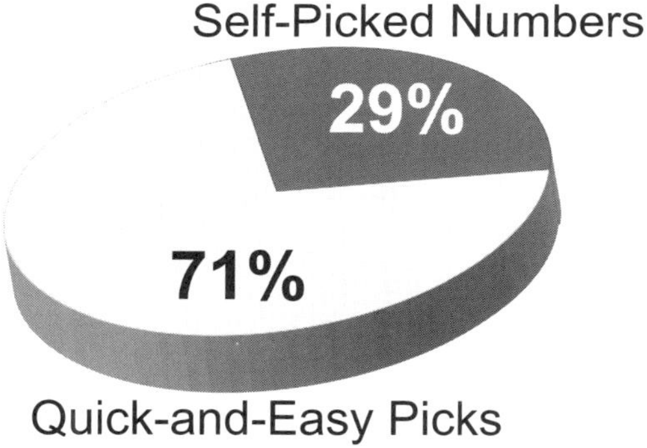

Lottery winners often cite "regular play" as being the key to lotto success. Ileana Rodriguez of Marietta, Georgia, won a multi-million dollar LOTTO SOUTH® jackpot after playing the same numbers for a decade. "We've never missed a big lotto drawing since the Georgia Lottery began 10 years ago," she said.[9]

MYTH 3

Most Lottery Players are Financially Poor

This myth persists even though it has been proven again and again that people who play lotteries are not those within the low-income sector. Rather, they are the ones who make up the middle class economic group.

According to the Office of Survey Research at the University of Texas:

Fact: The "typical" lottery player makes over $30,000 per year in personal income

Fact: A greater proportion of lottery players earn more than $50,000 annually.[10]

FIGURE 1.3

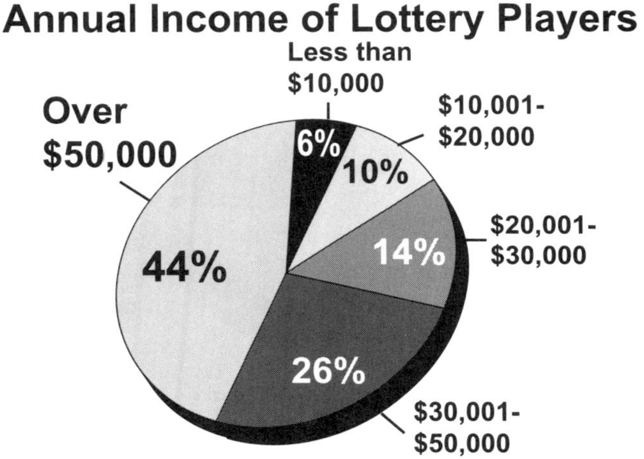

Another study between the Minnesota State Lottery and St. Cloud State University identified the 20 percent of lottery players reporting the highest expenditures. Of these lottery players, 96 percent had incomes of $15,000 or *more*, and 32 percent reported incomes of more than $50,000.[11]

A third corroborating poll found that people with incomes in excess of $75,000 spend roughly three times as much on lotteries each month as do those with incomes under $25,000.

MYTH 4

Only Uneducated People Play Lottery Games

Contrary to popular belief, it is not the least educated who play the lottery. In an about-face, people with the smallest amount of education are the least likely to play lottery games while those with higher educations are more likely to play. According to the Office of Survey

Research at the University of Texas, "College graduates and those with some college education (35 and 28 percent respectively) [are] the most likely to play lottery games" (2001).

Fact: 63% of Texas lottery players either have some college or a college degree

Fact: Only 9% of the lottery playing population has less than a high school education.[12]

FIGURE 1.4

Lottery-Player Education Level

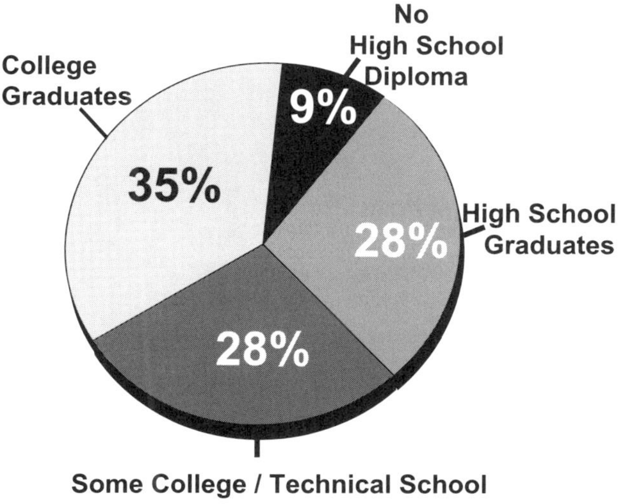

Time and again it is found that the more education a person has, the more likely he or she is to play lottery games. The Minnesota State Lottery and St. Cloud State University found that 88 percent of lottery players have at least a high school degree. The study also revealed that more than half of lottery players have some post-high school education.[13]

MYTH 5

Lotteries Prey on Minority Ethnic Groups

Ethnic group participation in lottery games reflects that of population rates. Of the estimated 171 million (FIGURE 1.7) people who play lottery games in the U.S., approximately 109 million are Caucasian, 42 million are Hispanic, and 15 million are African American.

Fact: 12.9% of the U.S. Population is African-American

Fact: 9% of Lottery Players are African-American

FIGURE 1.5

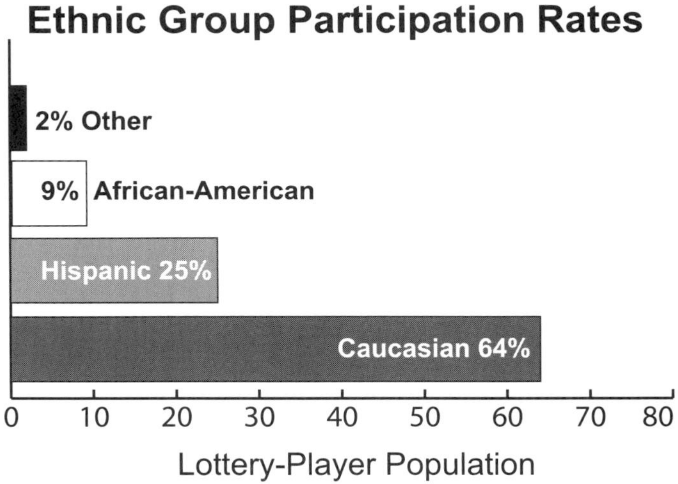

According to the Office of Survey Research at the University of Texas, "there is very little difference among ethnic groups concerning the incidence with which each plays Texas Lottery games, in relation to representation."[14] Lottery player participation rates found in FIGURE1.5 correspond with the diversity of the population during the same period of time (1996).

MYTH 6

The Lottery-Winner Curse

The "lottery-winners' curse" is a myth based on a belief that any form of gambling is an "electrifying unnatural yearning for gain." In accordance with this philosophy, people who win lottery jackpots are soon ruined by overindulgence because they are not disciplined enough to manage such a windfall. While jealousy may be the root of this myth, the reality is that most lottery winners become very conservative with their new wealth.

Fact: The lottery-winner's curse is a superstition

FIGURE 1.6

Common Reasons for Bankruptcy

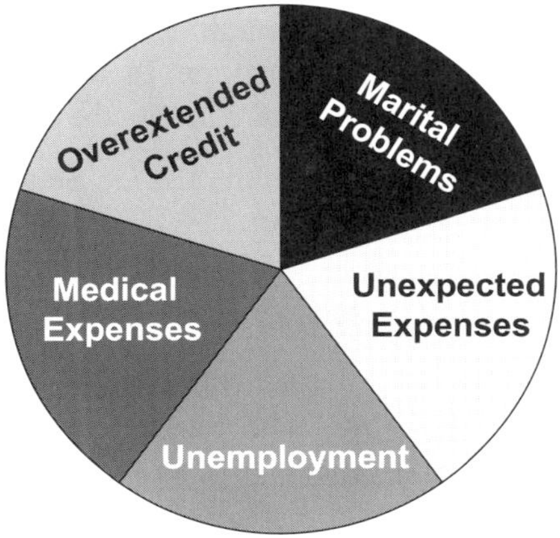

The problem with such mythical stories of lottery winners going bankrupt within five years, leaving a spouse within one year, developing horrific vices, or even committing suicide is that they are a product of sensationalism, the stories are unsubstantiated, and they fly in the face of the truth. Sure, there are lottery winners who have suffered such tragedies, but there is no evidence to suggest that one causes the other.

The only meaningful evidence reveals that lottery winners most commonly retire from employment, buy a new home, get rid of burdensome debt, lead a financially conservative lifestyle, and enjoy the qualities of life that big bucks make possible.

MYTH 7

Very Few People Actually Play Lottery Games

Stranger than fiction, the truth is that the vast majority of Americans play lottery games. Lottery games, which make-up an estimated $42 billion industry (2003), is one of the most popular forms of gambling and entertainment in the United States. Through pocketbook votes, Americans continue to demonstrate their approval of lotteries and the collective social benefits they afford.

Fact: 293 million people live in the United State of America (2004 est., U.S. Census).[15]

Fact: 266 million Americans reside in the 41 states and provinces with lottery games (2004 est. U.S. Census).[16]

Fact: Over 171 million Americans participate in a lottery game each year (2004 est.).

It is amazing to consider that out of the 266 million people who live in jurisdictions with lotteries, more than 64% buy at least one lottery ticket each year. The sheer number of people who purchase lottery tickets illustrates its popularity.

FIGURE 1.7

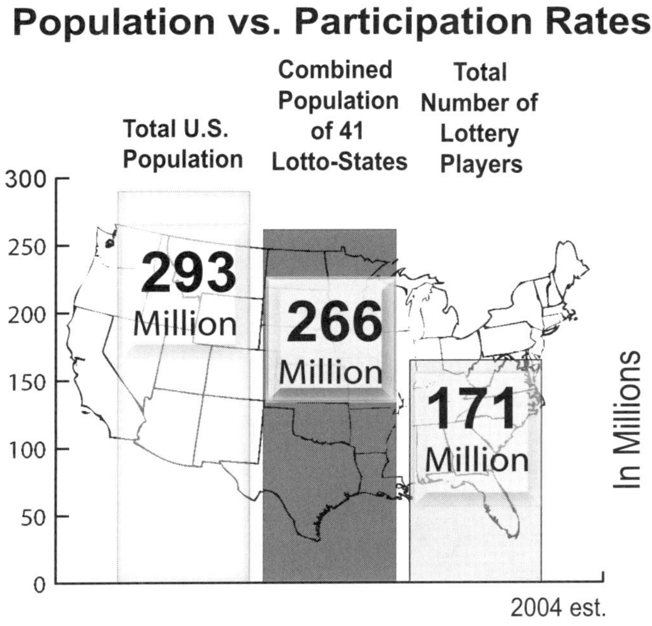

A March 2004 Gallup Poll found that "two in three Americans [66%] say they have participated in some form of gambling activity in the last 12 months, with state lotteries being the most common."[17] This finding is similar to the 70% of United Kingdom's population that plays their National Lottery.

Nevertheless, the Office of Survey Research at the University of Texas found that 63% of Texas adults have played the lottery at least once in the previous year.[18] And a 2003 study found that 69% of all Minnesota adults have played a lottery game during the previous 12months.[19] Such mirroring results from national and southern and northern regional polls make it reasonable to conclude that such characteristics are reflected nationwide.

- **Have You Ever Gambled?**

The April 2003 joint study between the Minnesota State Lottery and Social Science Research Institute at St. Cloud State University not only supports lottery

FIGURE 1.8

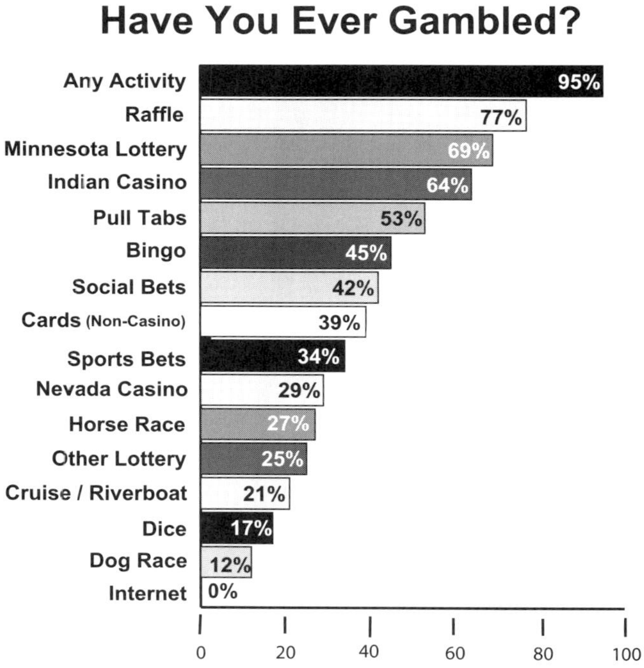

participation rates, but it also deflates the stereotype of the typical gambler. If you have ever purchased a raffle ticket in support of a community function or removed a contest pull-tab from the side of a soft drink cup, then you have gambled. Mirrored in other states, did you know that:

Fact: 95% of Minnesota adults have gambled at sometime during their lives.[20]

Fact: 83% of Minnesota adults have gambled in the year prior to the survey.[21]

Fact: In 2003, more residents played the Minnesota State Lottery than any other form of gambling in the state.[22]

Recent findings have revealed that 95% of those responding to the survey reported participating in at least one of the 16 forms of gambling available to Minnesota adults sometime during their lifetime.[23]

With lotteries remaining at the top of games-of-choice and the bottom for compulsive gamblers, the gambling and entertainment industry as a whole continues to be an American tradition.

Purchasing Habits by Gender

Demographic studies of lottery players continue to find that purchasing habits of lottery tickets between the male and female gender are quite similar. With a variation between studies of less than 5% and like-margin of errors, it cannot be definitively concluded that either gender purchases lottery tickets more than the other.

Even the Office of Survey Research at the University of Texas was only able to find a 2% difference in purchasing habits (Males 49% and Females 51%).[21] The Minnesota State Lottery's February 2004 Report only revealed a 5% gender difference.[22]

FIGURE 2.1

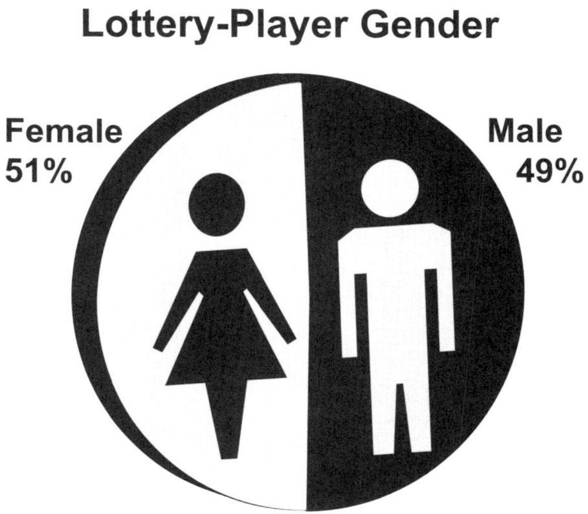

Age Requirement to Purchase Lottery Tickets

Age requirements to purchase lottery tickets in the United States can vary from state to state. In most states the lottery player must be at least 18 years of age. Some jurisdictions require the player to be 19 while others insist that you be 21 to claim a prize.

Age confirmation is one reason why lottery tickets cannot be purchased over the Internet. If the age requirement is problematic, you should contact an authorized retailer or your lottery agency for details.

Where to Purchase Lottery Tickets

Lottery tickets can be purchased 7 days a week from one of more than 250,000 authorized retailers in 41 states. Convenience stores, variety retailers and grocery stores are often authorized lottery retailers.

Due to federal interstate commerce laws, postal regulations and varying state laws, lottery tickets cannot be purchased over the telephone or internet. The Wire Communications Act of 1961 prohibits the use of wire communication facilities (telephone lines) for interstate or foreign gambling purposes.

Purchasing Annuity or Cash Option Tickets

At the time of purchase, the lottery player has the option of requesting either the annuity option or the cash option. Depending on the option selected, the lottery winner will either receive his/her prize in one lump sum, the "cash option", or they will receive annual payments, the "annuity option", for a specified number of years.

The cash-optioned ticket will bring the lottery winner a one-time payment of approximately half the advertised jackpot. The annuity-optioned ticket will bequeath between 20 and 30 annual payments that equal the entire advertised jackpot (see Finance Department).

Due to recent changes in the Internal Revenue Code, some lottery agencies allow the claimant to freely select their payment option of choice during the claims process. Other lottery agencies, such as in the State of Georgia, permit the annuity opted ticket to be changed to the cash option but not vice versa. Lottery players who want to keep their options "open" should select the annuity option when purchasing tickets.

Methods of Payment to Purchase Lottery Tickets

The method of payment accepted for lottery tickets varies among states. Cash or coin is the most popular forms of payment while paying by debit or credit card is less common.

In South Carolina, for instance, cash is the only method of payment accepted while credit cards, checks and debit cards are strictly prohibited. Lottery retailers in Iowa are permitted to accept coin, cash, checks and debit cards. Minnesota allows retailers to accept coin, cash, debit card and money orders for lottery ticket purchases.

Since credit cards are deferred methods of payment, few jurisdictions allow them to be used to purchase lottery tickets. Oregon and New Hampshire are among the few that permit retailers to accept credit cards.

Purchasing Lottery Tickets for Future Drawings

Purchasing lottery tickets in advance can be accomplished in a couple of ways. In a few states, lottery players can subscribe to or purchase season tickets. This option, which has yet to become a consumer trend, allows the lottery player to subscribe to a specific game using the same set of numbers for a specified number of draws.

In Virginia, Massachusetts and New York, for example, the lottery-ticket subscriber must provide an in-state mailing address and complete a subscription form. Discounts are often given to the season ticket customer. The cancellation of subscription or season lottery tickets is usually prohibited.

More common though, is the *multiple draw* option. With this method, the number set and play options selected are played in each drawing for the entire length of the chosen multiple-draw term. And unlike the subscription or season ticket, the multiple draw option can be purchased at any authorized lottery retailer by simply using the multiple draw boxes in the playslip's margin.

In most cases, the multiple draw option, also known as ADVANCE PLAY®, allows the lottery player to purchase tickets in advance for up to 10 consecutive drawings, depending on the game. The "multi-draw" option can be taken with either quick-and-easy picks or personally selected numbers.

Group Purchases of Lottery Tickets

Lottery pools are often created by co-workers, groups of friends, families and clubs and are believed to enhance the lottery playing experience. While groups can legally purchase lottery tickets, the fact that only a few states provide the multi-claimant option makes it difficult for many lottery-pools to claim their prize (see Claims Department).

Where group claims are prohibited, the standard procedure is for a single group member to claim the jackpot using his/her social security number. The problem occurs when trying to divide the winnings and tax liability. Not only does the tax responsibility fall completely on the individual claimant, but gift taxes can substantially reduce each member's "piece of the pie".

To avoid this dilemma, lottery-pools should obtain a Federal Employer Identification number FEIN from the IRS. By claiming the jackpot with an FEIN, each group member can be responsible for their share of the tax burden (see Tax Department, IRS Tax Forms).

Next, lottery pools should enter into a legal partnership agreement. While oral contracts can potentially be upheld in the division of lottery winnings, it is always best to define partnerships in writing. Simple partnership agreements with an attorney's "stamp of approval" can prevent disputes and court battle from ever taking place.

Canceling Lottery Tickets

While the policies of states and games differ, lottery tickets, for the most part cannot be cancelled. The accuracy of lottery tickets is the player's sole responsibility.

Especially in multi-state games, such as MEGA MILLIONS®[23], POWERBALL®[24], or LOTTO SOUTH®[25], lottery tickets cannot be cancelled. If a lottery ticket is printed incorrectly and fails to meet validation requirements (See Claims Department Validation Process), the purchaser has the right to decline the erroneous ticket. Erroneous lottery tickets are those printed in error by the sales clerk, those with printing irregularities, or those with illegible markings. However, this does not mean that the ticket is necessarily cancelled.

When a consumer discontinues a lottery ticket transaction, the clerk either purchases the mistake-ticket(s) himself, sells the ticket to future players, or returns it to the storeowner who becomes the ticket's rightful owner. Lottery agencies have strict rules about giving retailers credit for mistake tickets.

Nevertheless, on more than one occasion, unbought mistake-tickets have made clerks and/or storeowners lottery winners. Because of this, some strategists suggest that lottery players accept and purchase mistake-tickets as long as they meet validation requirements. Using playslips and good communication skills can help lottery players avoid the mistake-ticket nuisance.

Sales Department

Who Can Sell Lottery Tickets

Lottery commissions are finicky about whom they authorize to sell lottery tickets. For instance, some states, such as Tennessee (Tenn. Code Annot. §4-51-115), do not allow pawnshops or loan companies to sell lottery tickets. In most jurisdictions, the retailer cannot be exclusively engaged in the sole business of selling lottery tickets. Furthermore, authorized retailers cannot sell tickets from mobile or residential locations without obtaining explicit permission from the host lottery agency.

Businesses that wish to sell lottery tickets must submit an application and processing fee. After the background check is successfully completed and licensing requirements are met, the business becomes an authorized lottery retailer.

Communicating with Sales Agents

When purchasing lottery tickets it is important to effectively communicate your needs to the retailer. Good communication skills should always be used when purchasing lottery tickets, as they are often sold by young adults and/or non-native-speaking sales clerks whose communication skills have yet to be honed.

The recommended method of communicating your lottery-ticket needs is to use playslips, which are provided by the retailer. By using the playslip instead of making an oral request to the retailer, the lottery player can communicate directly with the Lottery's computer terminal without involving the sales clerk.

Using playslips is especially important for players who are hearing impaired, mute or suffering from a speech impediment.

Dishonest Sales Agents

While the deceitful sales agent is a rarity, it is always a good idea to be attentive when purchasing lottery tickets or claiming a prize. Monitoring the transaction and using good communication skills are the best ways to prevent misdeeds.

At the time of purchase the lottery player should confirm that the ticket(s) is not outdated and is for the specified drawing. Incorrect tickets should be exchanged prior to leaving the retailer's location.

The retailer's lottery computer terminal has the ability to recognize and validate winning tickets. However, it is NEVER a good idea to give complete responsibility for ticket-validation to anyone. Lottery players should check their tickets with reliable sources (i.e., televised drawings, lottery websites and hotlines and newspapers) instead of entrusting the task to others. Even prize amounts for non-jackpot winning tickets should be known before submitting tickets to retailers.

In the unlikely event you encounter wrongful behavior by a retailer, it is important to notify the lottery agency's Security and/or Fraud Department. Reporting fraud is not only socially responsible, but also the civic duty of every lottery player and victim. In addition to losing their license to sell lottery tickets, retailers who intentionally deceive lottery players can be prosecuted.

When allegations of fraud are substantiated and the retailer and/or sales clerk has intentionally deprived the lottery-player of winnings in excess of $100.00, the defendant may be charged with felony grand larceny. To prevent fraud, lottery agencies are extremely cautious with who they authorize to sell tickets and are proactive in performing audits and investigating claims of wrongdoing.

Selling Future Annuity Payments

Annuity-opted lottery winners commonly receive offers from third party investors to purchase some or all-remaining prize payments. While divesting or "selling off" future annuity payments may be legal, the practice is discouraged by unbiased financial experts.

In many instances, such "pawn shop" annuity investment companies will misrepresent themselves by claiming some sort of affiliation with the lottery agency or having the organization's endorsement. Lottery agencies *do not* endorse such brokers nor do they disclose non-public information. So, don't fall into their trap.

What some agencies do sanction, however, is the acceleration of annuity payments upon the lottery winner's death. Instead of "selling off" the annuitant's winnings, it may be possible for beneficiary(s) to withdraw the principal from the lottery investment. In jurisdictions that allow divesting, the lottery winners' "Estate" petitions the agency's investment division and requests that the principal be released in full. When the petition is granted, the remaining funds used to finance the annuity are disbursed in a final lump sum payment.

Shipping Department

Mailing / Shipping Lottery Tickets

Mailing or shipping lottery tickets is NEVER a good idea. As bearer instruments, lottery tickets are the property of whoever possesses and/or signs them. In the event a winning ticket is lost or destroyed, there would be no recourse or way to collect what is rightfully yours. Not to mention that by doing so you would be breaking federal law and can be fined and/or imprisoned.

According to federal law (18 USC 1301), importing or transporting lottery tickets through express companies or common carriers, is illegal.

> Whoever brings into the United States for the purpose of disposing of the same, or knowingly deposits with any express company or common carrier for carriage, or carries in interstate or foreign commerce any … instrument purporting to be or to represent a ticket, … or dependent upon the event of a **lottery**…or, [is] engaged in the business of procuring for a person in one

> State such a ticket, ... or interest in a **lottery** ...conducted by another state..., or knowingly takes or receives any such instrument... in interstate or foreign commerce ... for the purpose of procuring such a ticket... shall be fined under this title or imprisoned not more than two years, or both (18 USC 1301).

Mailing lottery tickets through the U.S. Postal Service is also against the law. According to United States Code, Title 18-Crimes and Criminal Procedure, Part I.-Crimes, Chapter 61,

> Whoever knowingly deposits in the mail, or sends or delivers by mail: ... any lottery ticket or part thereof, or paper, certificate or instrument purporting to be a ticket... any newspaper circular, or publication containing any advertisement of any lottery... shall be fined under this title or imprisoned not more than two years, or both; and for any subsequent offense shall be imprisoned not more than five years (18 USC 1302).

Lottery players should beware of foreign lotteries that advertise their games in the United States. Without exception, these lotteries are scams and should not be bought into. The Federal Trade Commission encourages consumers to give any suspicious "lottery" material from a foreign country to a local postmaster.

3 Psychology Department

Money and Happiness

Money is not merely a 2½ x 6-inch piece of paper with the face of a former president stamped on it; it is also a tool that helps us fulfill needs, wants and desires. While we certainly enjoy the adventure, excitement and self-accomplishment of being able to afford a new home, automobile or vacation, money brings us happiness and security in a wide variety of ways.

With money we can buy food, shelter, medical care, transportation, prenatal care or cancer treatment, funeral services, political or social cause promotion, quality education, or even trendy sneakers for a child craving social acceptance. Money is so important that it has even been declared by the courts to equal free speech; so money really does talk! By providing us with a means to meet our needs and enhance our standard of living, money can be viewed as a vehicle to happiness.

Money also brings us happiness through psychological advantage. It has been found that financially affluent people are psychologically healthier because they are able to put forth more effort towards achieving personal goals, enjoying peace of mind, giving back to their community, and doing good deeds.

Allocating more time for self-reflection and/or improvement, spending more time with family, children, and friends, and pursuing personal interests or hobbies have been found to reduce stress and improve mental health. So if money were not responsible for bringing some form of happiness, then why is it that people of wealth usually live longer and fuller lives?

Initial Lottery-Winner Reactions

Of all the emotional roller coasters to be ridden, hitting a multimillion-dollar jackpot is one of the most powerful and moving experiences conceivable. Since in many ways the human body cannot distinguish between good and bad emotions, the physiological responses that take place upon receiving extraordinarily good news or heart-wrenching bad news are in many ways the same.

In scientific terms, the first reaction of every lottery winner is the same, the release of dopamine in the cerebral cortex of the brain. Dopamine is a chemical naturally produced in the body and is associated with the unpleasant and "pleasure system" of the brain. As a stimulant, dopemine is responsible for the desire and pleasure of any rewarding experience (e.g. food, sex, winning a lottery jackpot). From this chemical reaction, the lottery winner will have an emotional respone.

The common emotions people initially go through after realizing they have won a multimillion-dollar lottery include those of extreme anxiety, bliss, numbness, fear, nervousness and/or disbelief.

From these responses the lottery winner may find himself stunned, sitting and staring, unable to speak, crying, screaming, weak-kneed, frantic and/or looking for emotional support. Lottery winners often suffer from sleeplessness and/or loss of appetite. Each lottery winner will go through a unique set of these emotions and react to the experience differently. The individual's maturity level is a factor in how he/she reacts to the discovery of being a lottery winner.

When Ileana Rodriguez realized she had won a $22 million LOTTO SOUTH® [29] jackpot in February of 2003, she frantically began calling her adult children and a friend to have them double-check that she had the winning set of numbers[30]. And when Jack Whittaker won the POWERBALL® [31] jackpot in December of 2002, he and his wife sat in their living room stunned with disbelief and didn't utter a word for nearly an hour.

And when Jerry Berggren, the March 27, 2002 POWERBALL® [32] jackpot winner of $48.1 million, telephoned his fiancée with the good news, she thought he was playing an April Fool's Day prank and refused to believe that he had actually hit the jackpot. After convincing her that he had actually won, she recalled hanging up the telephone, crying, vomiting and beginning to hyperventilate[33].

According to Mr. Berggren, "I was shaking the whole time I was driving home." Once home, Berggren's fiancée, Cathy DeMuynck, told him "You don't just call someone with news like that!" But he said he wanted her to know he had the winning ticket in case something happened to him on the way home[34].

False-Positive Winning Errors

There's a reason lottery winners commonly react with disbelief and frantically seek confirmation of the winning numbers. It is a natural tendency to second-guess such good fortune because of the possibility of a false-positive error. Not only do we want to protect ourselves from the humiliation of screaming "Bingo" and being wrong, but the lottery winner may not believe his/her own eyes.

A false-positive error, which occurs when a person believes they have won a lottery jackpot, but due to incorrect information actually have not, is a fear that causes lottery winners to frantically seek confirmation from others they trust.

Televised lottery drawings, lottery hotlines, newspapers and lottery-agency websites can individually and collectively be used to confirm lottery results. It is always a good idea to check more than one source.

Initial Reactions and Ticket Handling

As difficult as it may be, it is critical for the jackpot winner to remember that lottery tickets are bearer instruments and irreplaceable. In the course of your initial shock, you could find yourself running into another room to share the news or looking for assistance in confirming the winning set of numbers with the ticket clasped in your hand. Beware that it could be a knee jerk reaction for a family member or friend to grab at the ticket causing it to rip, drift into an unreachable location, or even worse, send it twirling into a flushing toilet. For these reasons and more it is imperative that you control your excitement and react cautiously.

After realizing you have a winning lottery ticket, you should immediately confirm that the backside of the ticket is filled-out and signed. If the ticket has yet to be filled-out and signed, it is important that you calmly do so and then put it in a secure place (see Security Department). By signing the ticket, it ceases to be a bearer instrument and becomes your legal property.

If away from home, the ticket should be secured on your person. It would be tragic to hit a lottery jackpot and lose the ticket to a gust of wind, a car thief or a purse-snatcher. Also when away from home, the lottery winner, who is in such an emotional state, should telephone a family member, a friend, or a taxicab to ensure a safe return home. As always, your safety and the safety of others is of the utmost importance.

Initial Reactions and Keeping Quiet

From the moment the winning ticket is realized until the claims process has been completed, lottery winners should not reveal their good fortune. For the sake of privacy, safety and planning, lottery winners should only tell those who need to know and who can be trusted to maintain confidentiality.

Historically, lottery winners who give into temptation and announce their good fortune have found themselves bombarded by the news media, investors, charities and beggars before they were prepared to claim the jackpot and answer questions. As the number of people who know of your lottery win increases, so does your privacy and security risk; so mum's the word.

Initial Reactions and Health Issues

Another immediate concern for the individual with a winning lottery ticket is his/her health and the well being of family and friends. It is a good idea for the lottery winner with a health condition to seek medical attention as soon as possible. And it is widely known in the medical profession that family members or friends in poor health should only be given exciting information if their condition can survive the news. You don't want to give old Aunt Martha a heart attack, do you?

Since most lottery officials are on the lookout for health-related problems during the claims process, it is not uncommon for them to inquire as to how the lottery winner(s) is feeling mentally, physically and emotionally. They will usually question the amount of sleep and/or food the lottery winner has had and may even offer a snack or meal.

The Impact of Retirement on Lottery Winners

One issue that consumes many lottery winners is the decision to continue or resign a career. The nature of this psychological dilemma often depends on the value placed on one's occupation. While many jackpot winners have no reservations about quitting work, others who have worked hard in their profession often find themselves going through the same emotional stages as people who face retirement.

Part of this is due to the amount of investment placed in education, training and building a career. Changing the habit of getting up every day and going to work is difficult and even harder for the lottery winner who has spent a lifetime in their vocation. For one reason or another, many lottery winners sincerely believe they will remain in their current job.

It usually doesn't take long, though, for the lottery winner to change his or her mind. After realizing it is unnecessary to work in order to maintain a certain standard of living, lottery winners often retire or start their own business. As usual, with retirement comes the question of "what next?"

Instead of retiring to sleep or watch television, psychologists suggest that the retiree use his/her free time to pursue a hobby, personal interests, social or political causes, or participate in community activities. By unfreezing the old habits and refreezing a new dynamic lifestyle, the lottery winner can enjoy the happiness that comes with having money.

Sudden Wealth Syndrome

Is it true that people hate any change that doesn't jingle in their pocket? The fact is that even a change for the better can be overwhelming and difficult to accept. When people, such as lottery winners, inherit large fortunes without warning they are susceptible to a psychological disorder known as Sudden Wealth Syndrome. Common symptoms include insomnia, anxiety, depression, denial and even guilt.

San Francisco psychologist Joan Difuria specializes in Sudden Wealth Syndrome, which has brought her national attention. "Like the well-known stages of grief following a death, the quick acquisition of wealth has its own stages," said Difuria, who works with colleague Mark Goldbart at the Money Meaning & Choices Institute[35].

According to the distinguished psychologist, lottery winners initially experience the "euphoric honeymoon… [which is] followed by a period of integrating their lives with their new financial state. The most responsible then enter a stage of stewardship, concentrating on long-term goals for themselves, their families and possibly their communities."[36]

Difuria also asserts that the publicity and attention lottery winners receive is a contributing factor to the psychological disorder. "When people don't expect it and haven't planned for it, they aren't ready for the bombardment of people coming to them."[37]

Goldbart and Difuria's three-stage treatment plan was developed to assist the unexpectedly wealthy in coping with Sudden Wealth Syndrome. The first step is to come to terms with the surprise, excitement, and confusion of sudden wealth. Secondly, the instant millionaire should work towards regaining a sense of control and comfort. The final step is to set personal priorities and goals. Difuria suggests that the lottery winner "take a deep breath and make wise decisions"[38]

4 Planning Department

Dreaming of Winning the Lottery

To dream about money while sleeping can mean a variety of things. From financial security to a warning to spend cautiously to a sign that an unexpected financial windfall is looming, many dream theorists believe that dreaming about money and how it is gained or lost is a prophetic vision.

> Salem, Ind. --- Tim Rivers had a dream last Tuesday night [March 9, 2004] that he'd won $200 million in the lottery. Rivers, 23, of Salem, who'd been laid off recently, told his family about the dream. They laughed at him. Rivers said he told his wife, "Why can't that happen to us?" It did. Mr. Rivers and his wife, Pam, were the only winners of Saturday's [March 13, 2004] $89 million Powerball® jackpot.[39]

Daydreaming, on the other hand, is a conscious *plan* and vision of an ideal situation that we naturally involve ourselves in while awake. Sigmund Freud (1908), the renowned psychoanalyst, defined daydreaming as a "wish-fulfillment" process and considered the natural act important to good mental health.

Scientists believe that the release of dopamine in the brain is responsible for the pleasure we feel when planning an exciting occurrence, such as a celebratory dinner or the possibility of "hitting a lottery jackpot". Considered to be a "reward chemical", the firing of dopamine neurons occurs when a pleasurable activity is expected, regardless of whether it actually happens or not. It is this chemical reaction that makes dreaming of winning a lottery jackpot an enjoyable and healthy experience.

Daydreaming about what you would do with millions of dollars from a lottery win is not only healthy, but it's a common method of tension-release and directly related to how you are planning the future. It is also what makes playing lottery games entertaining to 171 million people every year!

Dreamt Plans vs. Actual Plans

Inheriting a large sum of money is a monumental life-changing event, which affects everyone differently. With few exceptions, specific plans made during lottery daydreams rarely become reality for lottery winners. Like any dreamt ideal situation, when it actually happens the person does not react or carry out the envisioned occurrence precisely how he/she had imagined.

It is interesting to note that most lottery winners become very conservative and protective of their newfound wealth. Instead of the envisioned plan of buying the elaborate mansion, the massive yacht, the $100,000 diamond necklace, the $200,000 sports car and the two-year tour of Europe, lottery winners in general purchase only modest assets. A vacation home, reasonably priced luxury cars, and a few travels abroad are the most common purchases among lottery winners.

Plan to Avoid Lotto-Winner Bankruptcy

The key to avoiding lotto-winner bankruptcy is to exit the lottery winners' honeymoon as soon as possible, set realistic goals and stick to a solid financial plan.

According to Psychologist Joan DiFuria, "Often people who haven't had money overestimate what they can do with it." "It's important to get people's fantasies and realities lined up."[40]

In doing so, the lottery winner should employee a professional advisor who is trained and experienced in setting realistic fiscal goals and a comprehensive financial plan. In addition to helping you with these tasks, the Private Financial Manager (PFM) can assist you in other areas of planning too. He/she can help you with negotiations, contractual agreements, insurance assessment, tax filings and estate planning.

Before you invest in any large-scale assets, such as a home, jewelry or a sports car, you should discuss such purchasing plans with your advisor. Using a qualified PFM is how the financially affluent stay wealthy (see Human Resource Department).

Plan for the Claims Process

To provide time for planning and set-up, lottery jackpots are most often claimed anywhere from 4 days to 4 weeks after the lottery drawing. By postponing the claim, the much needed time to consult professional advisors, develop plans, set-up bank accounts, prepare for the press conference, and implement privacy / security controls is provided. But for the sake of security and claim periods, the delay should not be any longer than necessary.

While the claims process may be simple and quick, there are more than a few issues the lottery-winner needs to consider before, during, and after the event. In accordance with the wisdom that declares *by failing to prepare you are preparing to fail*, the prizewinner should develop a plan for claiming the jackpot so as to fully understand the decisions that will have to be made.

A *formal plan* to claim a lottery jackpot should consider various legal, financial, safety and personal issues, which are discussed throughout the remaining chapters of this book. Before claiming the lottery jackpot, the claimant(s) needs to think about and make decisions regarding such issues as:

- The Claims Process
- Hiring Interim and Permanent Advisors
- Lottery Policies, Rules, and Claims Procedures
- Transportation to Lottery Agency Headquarters
- Privacy & Security Needs
- Income Taxes
- The Cash or Annuity Payment Option
- Preparing for and Giving a Press Conference
- Immediate Banking Needs
- Giving to Family, Friends, and Charity
- AND MORE

Plan to Use Professionals in the Claims Process

Many lottery winners choose to use their annual Certified Public Accountant and neighborhood attorney in preparation for the claims process. When Mr. and Mrs. James Lewis won a $22.9 million POWERBALL® jackpot in August of 2000, he admitted to "…assembling a team of investment counselors, accountants and lawyers to advise his family on how to take the money, and what to do with it."[41]

In addition to preparations, many lottery winners feel more comfortable having these professionals with them during the claims process. Not only can they ensure that claim, beneficiary, and/or partnership forms are filled out correctly, but they can also help with press releases and interviews. Further, they can help set-up "special bank accounts" and monitor electronic fund transfers.

The lottery winner should work closely with their team of *interim* advisors. These professional relationships should be defined immediately and the parameters should be clearly stated, to wit, protection and assistance during the claims process, to setup for the immediate financial transactions, and to place the money in a secure and insured financial institution without binding constraints.

Remember that it is a good idea to reject any contracts, investments or accounts that obligate the prize money for more than a few months. While some short-term growth on the money may be sacrificed, at least hasty decisions or poor planning will not jeopardize the principal. This arrangement will give you time to employee the long term Private Financial Manager who is right for you (see Human Resource Department).

Whether or not to use interim professionals is a decision only the lottery winner can make. On the one hand, these professionals are easily accessible and can provide helpful services with short notice. On the other hand, there is an elevated risk in using the professional who lacks *all* the necessary skills and experience. Many lottery winners opt to delay their claim until the PFM is located and hired.

Planning to Quit Work

Some lottery winners are as eager to quit their job, as they are to collect their winnings. However, doing so too quickly could be a big mistake. First, it would be reckless to quit a position until the money is in the bank. Secondly, announcing your good fortune to co-workers before claiming the jackpot will increase your safety, security and privacy risks.

A better strategy is to simply take a little sick or vacation time off from work without mentioning your good fortune. If you are like the majority (>76%) of lottery winners and decide to quit your job, there will be plenty of time to submit a formal letter of resignation after you have gone public with the news.

Plan the Future of Prize Payments upon Death

Proper estate planning is of the utmost importance for lottery winners. In the event the lottery winner dies before collecting all annuity payments, a legal last will and testament will ensure that all assets, including future annuity payments, are passed on to his/her named beneficiaries. While lottery agencies *never* keep lottery winnings of the deceased, there are other legal and tax related issues that could jeopardize the winnings. For this reason, heirs should be named before or during the claims process.

Transportation Department

Traveling to Claim a Lottery Jackpot

Driving yourself to claim a multimillion-dollar lottery jackpot is not recommended. As noted by numerous claimants, the excitement and anxiety that comes with traveling with a winning jackpot ticket can be overwhelming and dangerous. Just as any other time, lottery winners should consider their own safety and the safety of others.

In preparing for the claims process, the jackpot winner should plan a safe and seamless route to the lottery headquarters or dedicated claims center. The route to be traveled should be mapped out so uncustomary safety and security measures can be taken. Avoidance of crime-ridden areas, traffic congestion and detours is the main idea behind planning the monumental "road-trip".

While the automobile is the most popular form of transit, it may be necessary for out-of-state claimants or those who do not drive to select another mode of transportation. In doing so, the lottery winner should use the safest type of transportation available. Other transportation issues such as weather, airport or rail station security, and hotel accommodations should also be considered.

The lottery winner traveling by air or rail should prearrange transportation between the airport or rail station and the lottery headquarters. To avoid the potential hazards, many lottery winners hire executive transportation services for the claims process. But regardless of how you get there, don't forget that no one needs to know or has the right to force you into divulging where and why you are traveling. It's a business trip, Period!

To enhance safety and reduce risk, lottery winners usually travel by the safest means available. TABLE 4.1 illustrates the Odds of Death Due to Injury, United States, 2001 as reported by the National Safety Council.[42] Statements about the odds or chances of dying from a given cause of death may be made as follows: Referring to the *second row* of TABLE 4.1:

- The odds of dying from a bicycle accident in 2001 were **1** in **359,967**
- The lifetime odds of dying from a bicycle accident for a person born in 2001 were **1** in **4,663**

TABLE 4.1

Type of Accident By Mode	Deaths	One Year Odds	Life-time Odds
Walking	6,071	46,960	608
Bicyclist	792	**359,967**	**4,663**
Motorcyclist	3,042	93,719	1,214
Car	14,946	19,075	247
Bus	37	7,705,238	99,809
Railway Train	26	10,965,147	142,036
Boat	591	482,392	6,249
Airplane	918	310,560	4,023

The odds given above are statistical averages over the whole U.S. population and do not necessarily reflect the chances of death for a particular person from a particular external cause. Any individual's odds of dying from various external causes are affected by the activities in which they participate, where they live and drive, what kind of work they do, and other factors.[43]

- National Safety Council

Lottery Headquarters / Dedicated Claim Centers

When planning the trip to the lottery headquarters or claims center, the lottery winner should also know the hours of operation and location of where jackpot tickets must be claimed. Claims appointments may be required. The following table provides the address and telephone number for all 41-lottery headquarters in the U.S.

TABLE 4.2

Arizona
4740 E. University Dr.
Phoenix, AZ 85034
(480) 921-4400

California
600 N. Tenth Street
Sacramento, CA 95814
(800) 568-8379

Colorado
Wells Fargo Building
201 W. 8th St., Suite 600
Pueblo, CO 81002
(719) 546-2400

Connecticut
270 John Downey Dr.
New Britain, CT 06051
(860) 348-4000

Delaware
McKee Business Park
1575 McKee Road
Dover, DE 19904
(302) 739-5291

District of Columbia
2000 14th Street, NW
Washington, DC 20009
(202) 671-2607

Florida
250 Marriott Drive
Tallahassee, FL 32301
(850) 487-7777

Missouri
1823 Southridge Drive
Jefferson City, MO 65102
(573) 751-4050

Montana
2525 North Montana Ave.
Helena, MT 59601-2525
(406) 444-5825

Nebraska
301 Centennial Mall South
14th & 'M'
Lincoln, NE 68509
(402) 471-6100

New Hampshire
14 Integra Drive
Concord, NH 03301
(603) 271-3391

New Jersey
One Lawrence Park
Brunswick Avenue Circle
Lawrenceville, NJ 08648
(609) 599-5800

New Mexico
4511 Osuna Road NE
Albuquerque, NM 87199
(505) 342-7529

New York
One Broadway Center
Schenectady, NY 12301
(518) 388-3300

Georgia
250 Williams St., NW
Atlanta, GA 30303-1071
(404) 215-5000

Idaho
1199 Shoreline Lane
Boise, ID 83702
(208) 334-2600

Illinois
201 E Madison
Springfield, IL 62702
(217) 524-5155

Indiana (Hoosier)
201 South Capitol Ave.
Indianapolis, IN 46225
(317) 264-4800

Iowa
2015 Grand Ave.
Des Moines, IA 50312
(515) 281-7900

Kansas
128 N Kansas Avenue
Topeka, KS 66603
(785) 296-5700

Kentucky
1011 West Main Street
Louisville, KY 40202
(502) 560-1500

Louisiana
555 Laurel St.
Baton Rouge, LA 70801
(225) 297-2000

Maine
8 State House Station
Augusta, ME 04333
(207) 287-3721

Ohio
615 West Superior Avenue
Cleveland, OH 44113
(216) 787-3200

Oklahoma
3817 N. Santa Fe
Oklahoma City, OK 73118
(405) 521-0520

Oregon
500 Airport Road SE
Salem, OR 97301
(503) 540-1000

Pennsylvania
2850 Turnpike Ind. Drive
Middletown, PA 17057
(717) 986-4699

Rhode Island
1425 Pontiac Avenue
Cranston, RI 02920
(401) 463 - 6500

South Carolina
1333 Main Street 4th Floor
Columbia, S.C. 29201
(803) 737-2002

South Dakota
207 E. Capitol, Ste. 200
Pierre, SD 57501
(605) 773-5770

Tennessee
200 Athens Way, Suite 200
Nashville, TN 37228
(615) 253-6881

Texas
611 E. 6th Street
Austin, TX 78701
(800) 375-6886

Maryland
1800 Washington Blvd.
Baltimore, MD 21230
(410) 230-8800

Massachusetts
60 Columbian Street
Braintree, MA 02184
(781) 849-5555

Michigan
101 E. Hillsdale
Lansing, MI 48909
(517) 335-5756

Minnesota
2645 Long Lake Road
Roseville, MN 55113
(651) 297-7456

Vermont
379 South Barre Road
South Barre, VT 05670
(802) 479-5686

Virginia
900 E. Main Street
Richmond VA 23219
(804) 692-7000

Washington
814 4th Avenue E.
Olympia, WA 98506
(360) 664-4720 or 4750

West Virginia
312 McCorkle Avenue
Charleston, WV 25330
(304) 558-0500

Wisconsin
2135 Rimrock Road
Madison, WI 53708-8941
(608) 261-4916

All information found in the table above should be checked for accuracy before traveling to claim your lottery jackpot. Authorized lottery retailers, lottery agency websites and local telephone directories are excellent sources to confirm that the above information has not changed since the printing of this book (2006).

5 Claims Department

Claiming a Lottery Jackpot

A life of luxury may be a difficult pursuit for most, but for the owner of a winning lottery ticket, it's a breeze. With the exception of a few unwise claimants, lottery winners by and large are amazed at how simple the claims process really is. In the uncomplicated words of Ileana Rodriguez, the winner of a $22 million advertised jackpot, "Claiming a lottery ticket is easy… there are no lines, no waiting; we were just given a big check."[44]

Without a doubt, the most difficult part of the claims process is having the numbers on your lottery ticket match those selected for the particular drawing. Once this obstacle is hurdled, all that is left is a little preparation, some valuable planning, and a monumental road-trip to claim your lottery jackpot.

Deadlines to Claim Lottery Winnings

The deadline to claim lottery prizes depends on the claim period for the particular game. The claim period, which is the range of time starting with the date of the drawing and extending to the time in which the prize is forfeited, varies significantly. Claim periods for big-game lotteries, such as MEGA MILLIONS®, SUPERLOTTO PLUS®, LOTTO SOUTH® and POWERBALL®, range between 180 – 365 days from the date of the drawing.

In some states, an additional *payment-option claim period* is instituted. For instance, POWERBALL®

winners in Tennessee and Connecticut must decide how they want to be paid (30 year annuity or lump-sum) within 60 days of the drawing. Failure to meet the payment option deadline can mean you lose the option to freely select how you want to be paid.

And even though some lottery agencies may offer an appeals process, it is recommended that you plan ahead and claim your prize several days or even weeks before the inflexible deadline. In states that require claims appointments, the lottery winner should schedule the event leaving enough time to reschedule the meeting if necessary.

Estimated Time of the Claims Process

Claiming a lottery jackpot is a relatively quick process. The entire process usually takes less than an hour for the single claimant. Lottery winners who make appointments usually spend less time claiming their prize. To schedule a claims appointment, simply telephone the host lottery agency and ask for an appointment.

Factors such as computer failures, private discussion with legal counsel, giving a press conference, the amount of public interest and the size of the press pool can extend the length of the claims process.

A group or partnership claim may also extend the duration of the claims process. Since group members may have to fill-out individual claims forms or one comprehensive form, it will take longer for all claimants to complete the paperwork, as well as for lottery officials to process the additional information.

Identification Requirements

Lottery winners are required to provide at least two forms of identification when claiming a jackpot prize. A social security card and driver's license with your current address are common forms of *positive identification* that are accepted by lottery agencies. The purpose for this policy is so identity, legal age, citizenship and other legal requirements can be confirmed. In partnership claims, each group member of the claim will have to provide two forms of positive identification.

Claims Validation Process

The claims validation process begins with the submission of a winning lottery ticket to the lottery agency in the state or province where the ticket was purchased. While policies and procedures vary, all lottery agencies have strict validation requirements.

First, a tangible lottery ticket with the winning set of numbers for the specific drawing must be submitted--playslips are worthless and counterfeit tickets bring criminal charges. Lottery tickets that are altered, erroneous, unreadable or mutilated are disallowed from the claims process. The play symbols, captions, validation number, barcode, and retailer validation number must correctly appear on the winning ticket.

Before any claim is made on a jackpot, the Lottery's computer processing system will confirm where and at what time the ticket was sold. In comparison with this information, claimants are usually questioned as to where, when, and the circumstances in which the ticket was purchased. This practice is one of several methods used in validating the winning ticket(s).

The primary method of validation however, is the certification of the validation number. This number, which appears on each ticket, is entered into the Lottery's computer, which in turn identifies the ticket as a winner or non-winner. The validation number is also formatted as a bar code, which allows the electronic scanning of the validation number for faster processing.

Security-Guard Escort

In many cases, the claimant is assigned a security guard as an escort through the claims process. Most often, it is the security guard who will meet you at the reception area and usher you to the back-offices. Don't be surprised if the security guard stands by your side through the entire claims process and press conference. Having personal security is comforting for most lottery winners.

In instances where lottery winners have forgotten to bring the necessary documents, such as positive identification or the actual lottery ticket(s), agency security guards have been known to escort the claimant back to his/her home and ensure a safe return to lottery headquarters. Providing this type of personal care exemplifies the first-rate customer service found at lottery agencies.

Prize Money Collection

The essence of the claims process, which is collecting your multimillion-dollar prize, is what makes playing and winning the lottery worthwhile. Unlike the gift that is given in goodwill, the owner of a winning jackpot ticket receives payment on a debt. After the ticket's authenticity is validated, the lottery winner will receive his/her prize money.

Depending on the lottery game and the payment option selected, disbursement will be made either in a single check or a prescheduled series of annual checks. While some lottery agencies make the lump-sum payment available for pick-up, annuity checks are usually mailed to a specified address or electronically transferred into a financial account.

The exact length of time until the prizewinning is disbursed to the lottery winner differs between states and games. In some games, the lottery winner will receive his/her lump-sum check or the first of 20- 30 annual checks during the claims process. In others cases, the claimant will have to wait anywhere from one to six weeks before the prize money is distributed. An additional 5-day waiting period may be necessary for lottery agencies to arrange an electronic fund transfer (EFT) of the prize winnings to your specified financial institution.

Press Conference

Lottery winners are often invited to participate in an *optional* press conference following the validation of the winning ticket. These taped interviews however, are typically reserved for significantly large jackpots or "newsworthy" stories.

The press conference will either take place at the conclusion of the claims process, or will be scheduled to occur within a couple of days. Consisting of a small press-pool, the interview is a simple question-and-answer discussion of the claimant's personal lottery-winning experience. The entire event normally takes between 15 to 30 minutes.

More often than not, lottery winners find that giving a press conference enhances the winning experience. Interview tips, sample questions, and preparations for the lotto-winner press conference are discussed in the Public Relations Department.

The Claims Form

All jackpot winners are given a claims form at the beginning of the claims process. This document, which must be filled out completely, requires personal contact and identity information, a signature and the actual winning lottery ticket to be stapled to it.

Lottery winners should take special care in answering citizenship status questions on the claims forms. Failure to mark that you are a U.S. Citizen or resident alien will enact the 28% federal income tax premium which non-citizens have to pay on lottery winnings.

It is important for lottery winners to be aware that agency policies commonly prohibit claim forms from being changed once they have been submitted. The following example Claims Form illustrates the common attributes of the document.

State of Game

Lottery Claims Form

Staple Ticket Here

EXAMPLE

Instructions

- Fill out form in print
- Staple ticket to form
- Sign form
- Deliver To:........................ State of Game Lottery, 1557 Bon-Anna Road, Boro, State 10101

OFFICIAL LOTTERY USE ONLY

Retailer Name: ________________________________

Address: ________________________________

Lotto Merchant ID #: ________________________________

CLAIMS INFORMATION

Ticket Number: __________-__________-__________

Amount of Prize: $________________________________

Name of Lottery Game: ________________________________

Date Purchased: __________/__________/__________

Full Name: ________________________________

Address: ________________________________

City: ______________ State: ______ Zip Code: ________

Telephone: ( ) __________-____________________

U.S. Citizen: Yes No Resident Alien (circle one)

Gender: Male Female (circle one)

Social Security #:__________-__________-__________

Date of Birth: __________/__________/__________

I declare under penalty and perjury that all information on this form is accurate to the best of my knowledge. I am 18 years of age and understand that I must not use this form but rather an official claims form in the State where the ticket was purchased.

Winner's Signature: ________________________________

Date: ______/________/____________

The Group Claims Form

With few exceptions, lottery winners are notorious for demonstrating their generosity and/or loyalty to family, friends and lottery pool groups. Lottery pools are often created within families, groups of friends, or co-workers and can make playing and winning the lottery a more exciting experience.

But once the lottery is won, having to split the jackpot isn't the only burden that comes with group claims. For one, agency policies often disallow checks to be made out to more than one person. Other lotteries require that each claimant receive a minimum percentage, typically 1%, of the entire winnings. Some agencies place a minimum and/or maximum limit on the number of claimants who can participate in the group claim.

A third set of complications includes requirements such as each group member having to provide positive identification, fill out and sign Multiple Ownership claims forms, and complete a special tax form to split tax liabilities.

Some states only allow groups to claim a jackpot via a legal partnership with a federal identification number. And several states require the annuity option to be taken in instances of group claims. Good legal advice is essential for the group or partnership claim.

State of Game

Lottery Group Claims Form

Instructions *EXAMPLE*

- Complete boxes at top of form
- Complete one section for each person

Name of Game Won:	Ticket Number:
Amount of Prize Claimed:	**Ticket Holder Name:**
Date of Drawing:	**Date of Claim:**

The primary ticket holder agrees to share his/her winning with the individuals listed below and understands that the debt will be reduced accordingly.

I declare under penalty of perjury that all information given is accurate to the best of my knowledge. I am 18 years of age and understand that I must not use this form but rather an official Multi-Ownership claims form in the State where the ticket was purchased. Each claimant is responsible for his/her share of tax liability.

SS#:	Share %	Amount	SS#:	Share %	Amount

Ticket Holder Name__________
Date of Birth ____/____/______
Address ____________________
City, State, Zip______________
Signature ___________________

Shareholder Name________________
Date of Birth _____/____/_________
Address___________________________
City, State, Zip __________________
Signature_________________________

SS#:	Share %	Amount	SS#:	Share %	Amount

Shareholder Name ___________
Date of Birth ____/____/______
Address ____________________
City, State, Zip______________
Signature ___________________

Shareholder Name________________
Date of Birth_____/____/___________
Address___________________________
City, State, Zip____________________
Signature_________________________

SS#:	Share %	Amount	SS#:	Share%	Amount

Shareholder Name ___________
Date of Birth _____/___/______
Address_____________________
City, State, Zip______________
Signature

Shareholder Name________________
Date of Birth______/_____/________
Address___________________________
City, State, Zip __________________
Signature

The Claimant Survey Form

In an effort to collect survey data on "typical" lottery players and winners, lottery agencies often provide claimants with a short and straight-forward

State of Game

Lottery Winner Survey Form

EXAMPLE

General Information

Amount of Prize: $________________________.00
Name of Lottery Game: ______________________
Date Purchased: ________/__________/________
City of Purchase: __________________________
Type of Retailer: __________________________
Lottery Winner's Resident State: ______________

Please check or complete all that apply

1. Where do you mostly see advertising for this game?
Television____ Radio_____ Newspaper_____ Other _______

2. Of this type of game, how many tickets do you buy?
____(x) Tickets per: Day____ Week_____ Month______

3. In the previous 12 months, how often have you played this game? Daily_________ Weekly________ Monthly_______

4. How long have you played this lottery game? ______________

5. What is the highest level of school you have completed?
Less than high school_____ High school graduate _____
Technical School _____ Some College _____
College Degree _____ Advanced Degree _____

6. What is your current household income?
Up to $14,999 ____ $30,000 to $39,999____
$15,000 to $19,999____ $40,000 to $49,999____
$20,000 to $29,000____ $50,000 or more ____

7. What is your age group? 18 - 25___ 26- 39___ 40 – 49 ___
50 - 59___ 60- 69___ Over 70___

Control Number: 005687

multiple-choice questionnaire to complete. The survey form will contain between 5 and 20 inquiries, and will ask questions pertaining to your level of education, household income, frequency of play, and game-of-choice.

A control number is attached to the survey form so that personal information can be entered into a database for statistical analysis without direct correlation to the lottery winner.

Although optional, it is most certainly socially responsible to complete the questionnaire in an effort to help the lottery commission understand and measure advertisement effectiveness, player demographics and the impact on society.

The Beneficiary Form

Many lottery agencies provide forms for lotto-winners to name beneficiaries in the event of death before collecting all of their winnings. This legal form documents the individual(s) who will receive the remaining prize payments, should death occur.

Lottery winners who already have their estate planned should consult their attorney before signing the beneficiary form. On the other hand, it is important for those who do not have a will to name a beneficiary(s) during the claims process. This document will serve as a preliminary will until the Private Financial Manager is hired to plan the estate more carefully.

Claimants should bring their beneficiary's personal information, such as full name, address and social security number to the claims process. The following example Lottery Winner Beneficiary Form illustrates the typical contents of the document.

State of Game

Lottery Winner Beneficiary Form

EXAMPLE

Date: ____/____/____ Date of Drawing: ____/_____/_____

Name of Claimant / Benefactor: ___________________________

Date of Birth: ________/________/______________________

Social Security Number: ________-_________-__________

State of Residence: ______________________________________

City_________________, State______, Zip: _____________

Telephone Number: ______________________________________

Named Beneficiaries

Relation to Primary Beneficiary: ____________________

Name of Primary Beneficiary: __________________________

Social Security Number: ________-________-__________

Address:____

City_________________, State________, Zip: ___________

Relation to Contingent Beneficiary: _________________

Name of Contingent Beneficiary: ______________________

Social Security Number: _______-_________-__________

Address:____

City_________________, State______, Zip: _____________

Telephone Number: ______________________________________

I designate the named beneficiaries to receive my estate upon my death, etcetera, and etcetera. I am 18 years of age and understand that this is only an example beneficiary form and should not be used to legally name beneficiaries.

Claimant Signature: ______________________________

Unclaimed Prizes

Every year hundreds of millions of dollars in prize money goes unclaimed. Although unfortunate for the lottery winner(s), the prize pools of future lotteries are increased and socially responsible programs are better funded.

The most common reasons for lottery winnings going unclaimed include the ticket being lost or misplaced, submitted after the due date or accidentally destroyed. In other cases, illegal aliens or fugitives from justice have forgone a life of luxury to remain in the United States or out of jail.

While the distribution of unclaimed prize winnings differs between states and games, the norm is for the money to be returned to the general lottery fund and subsequently used for future drawings. Some lottery agencies set aside a small percentage of unclaimed prize money for additional lottery-game advertising, environmental protection, economic development, and/or education and treatment programs to combat gambling problems.

6 Finance Department

Take the Cash or Annuity Option?

Is a bird in the hand worth two in the bush?

According to 92% of POWERBALL® winners (1998-2002), the cash option, or a bird in the hand, is the payment option of choice. But despite its popularity, the lottery winner should be more concerned about taking the payment option that is right for him or her. To say the least, it would be foolish to take the lump-sum option without a good reason for accepting only half of the advertised jackpot. Instead, the lottery winner should take the advantages and disadvantages of each payment option into account before making a decision.

In deciding which payment option is right for you, it is important to consider such factors as the "honeymoon," the advertised jackpot, the tax burden and the age issue. You will also want to understand the differences between the cash and annuity-option. Lottery winners who owe back-taxes or child support payments will need to know how these debts affect the total prize.

When there are multiple jackpot winners, it is important to consider the dividing effects of splitting the prize and the impact it has on each payment option. Remember that all prizes for lotteries are *pari-mutual*. This means that the total prize amount is divided equally among all winners in that category.

Lottery-Winner Honeymoon

One of the initial stages the lottery winner goes through is the honeymoon. During this period, according to psychologist Joan Difuria, the lottery winner will enjoy a "top-of-the-world feeling," which often carries with it "impulses to spend and be generous."[45]

While the length of the honeymoon varies with winners of differing maturity levels, the size of the jackpot is a factor that influences the duration of the spending spree. But like all celebrations, the lottery winner's honeymoon must end, sooner or later.

According to Difuria, "The danger comes when someone gets stuck in the honeymoon period. If the honeymoon doesn't wear off, the money will be lost in two to five years[46]." She recommends purchasing things you've always wanted, but cautions against over doing it. One Florida lottery winner learned this lesson the hard way.

> Paul Scott Cooney was a 26-year old dispatcher at an Atlanta-area auto dealership in 1989 when he won $20 million in the Florida lottery. A decade later—after going through two divorces, five houses, a dozen cars and motorcycles and a failed auto dealership—he ended up in bankruptcy court.[47]

Had Mr. Cooney ended his honeymoon sooner and focused his attention on a sensible financial plan, his lotto-luck could have been different. So for the lottery winner who aspires to avoid the honeymoon-to-bankruptcy scenario, a dollar amount and time limit should be placed on the spending spree.

Selecting the annuity payment option is one way for lottery winners to avoid the destructive force of the overextended honeymoon. By limiting the festivities, this payment option also serves as a budgeting tool by guaranteeing a percentage of the winnings every year for 20-30 years.

Advertised Jackpot

The advertised jackpot is the dollar amount often publicized on billboards, television commercials and the lottery ticket itself. However, it is not simply the sum of lottery tickets sold, but rather a projected forecast of various market factors.

Historic sales trends, the weather, competing games and even current events that influence the spending habits of lottery players are used to project lottery jackpots. The ever-changing nature of these factors makes it difficult to predict the size of any jackpot with precise accuracy.

Tax Issue

It's not a question of whether your lottery winnings will be taxed, but rather when and by how much. While individual filing status, tax rates, and the size of the jackpot are all factors used in determining the amount of income tax owed, the payment option selected will ultimately frame how and when your winnings are taxed.

If the cash option is selected, taxes will be deducted from the entire prize immediately. And if the annuity option is chosen, the principal is allowed to grow without being taxed. Only the portion that is paid to the lottery winner each year incurs the state and/or federal income tax.

Age Issue

When it comes to selecting the payment option that is right for you, life expectancy rates should not be overlooked. According to the Central Intelligence Agency's World Fact Book, the average male can plan on living to the age of 74.5 years and the typical female will live to be 80.2 years old (2002 est.).[48] By comparing current age to life expectancy rates, the lottery winner can make a better-informed decision about what is right for him or her.

If current age plus the term of the annuity for the specific game exceeds the life expectancy rate, the lottery winner may be better off taking the cash option. And if current age plus the length of the annuity falls beneath the life expectancy rate, the annuity option is often preferred.

Based on the fact that the median annuity term is 26 years, males over the age of 48 and females over the age of 54 may get more benefit from the cash-option. Of course, the lottery winner's health condition and family medical history should be taken into account when using the age issue to make the payment option decision.

Annuity Payment Option

The annuity option may not be the most popular, but it certainly has its advantages. By accepting the annuity option, the lottery winner receives the amount invested by the lottery commission, the principal (aprx. ½ of the advertised jackpot), plus the interest earned over a specified number of years. The greatest benefit of the annuity option is that income tax is only withheld from the annual payment and not the entire principal.

It works like this. The lottery agency takes the money in the prize pool, the principal, and purchases government-backed investments, such as U.S. Treasury, Security, or Zero-Coupon bonds. In turn, the principal and accumulated interests of the bonds produce yearly returns until the annuity is fully matured and you have received the entire advertised jackpot.

Let's say the advertised jackpot for a big-game lottery is $10 million. In reality, the lottery agency actually has only about half, or $5 million, of that amount in the prize pool. When the claimant selects the annuity option, the lottery agency's investment department takes the $5 million and goes out and buys a $10 million government bond on the lottery winner's behalf.

Based on a lottery game that makes 26 annual payments to the winner, you will receive a first payment of $260,000 or 2.6% of the jackpot, minus taxes. As your principal grows over the next 25 years, so will your annual payment. Providing for inflation, your last and final lottery check would roughly amount to $520,000 or 5.2% of the advertised jackpot. After 26 years, at which time the bond is fully mature, you will have received the full $10 million.

The basic premise of the *annuity certain* is that half of the advertised jackpot is placed in an interest-bearing account, which defers the income tax and guarantees a fixed number of gradually increasing annual payments for the life of the annuity.

As important as it is to understand the mechanics of the annuity option, it is of equal substance to recognize some of the pros and cons in choosing it. For instance, many lottery winners are afraid that if they die before receiving all of their winnings that the remaining annuity payments will go uncollected. But, this couldn't be further from the truth. We already know that if a lottery winner dies before all annuity payments are received, the annuitant's beneficiaries will inherit the remaining annual payments.

Another benefit to the annuity option is that it can be used as collateral to secure loans from financial institutions. The annuity option gives lottery winners the opportunity for long-term investment and the ability to secure loans and fulfill present wishes.

A third advantage to the annuity option is that it helps lottery winners manage their winnings more effectively. Instead of assuming the responsibility of an *inheritor's fortune*, the annuity-payment option allows time between annual prize payments to make mistakes and learn from them, without jeopardizing the entire fortune. From adjusting to a new financial status to developing budgeting skills, the annuity option can act like a crutch and function as an allowance for the undisciplined lottery winner.

One disadvantage to the annuity option, which seems to weigh heavily on many lottery winners, is that all material needs and/or wants may not be fulfilled immediately. Instead, the annuity-opted lottery winner may have to plan, budget and wait for future payments in order to purchase expensive assets. Because of this, many jackpot winners lose sight of the annuity option's actual value and forfeit almost half of the prize.

Another disadvantage to the annuity option is that lottery winners over a certain age may not live long enough to enjoy the entirety of their good fortune. While some lottery winners see the annuity option as a protected and tax-deferring means of passing their estate on to loved ones, others find it more important to enjoy it while they can.

Cash-Payment Option

The cash option, also known as the lump-sum option, is the most popular payment method among lottery winners. This one-time cash payout is the actual amount of money in the prize pool that would otherwise be invested by the lottery agency on the claimant's behalf. Lottery winners who take the cash option receive approximately ½ of the advertised jackpot.

One advantage to the lump-sum payment is that the lottery winner is free to fulfill material needs and wants without delay. Total control over the principal is another benefit that is highly valued by many winners.

The most noteworthy disadvantage of the cash option is that the full advertised jackpot is forfeited. A lottery winner who wins a $10 million jackpot will receive about ½, or $5 million, of the advertised amount.

Another drawback is that income taxes are immediately withheld from the entire cash payout. For instance, a lottery winner in the State of Georgia who opts for the lump sum payment would immediately have federal income tax (currently 25%) and state income tax (currently 6%, 2004) withheld from the entire payment. The $10 million jackpot winner in the State of Georgia who takes the lump sum payment of $5 million would bring home approximately $3.45 million after federal and state income taxes (2004 est.).

When there are multiple jackpot winners, taking the cash option becomes even less advantageous. Depending if the pari-mutual jackpot is divided into halves, thirds, etcetera, taking the cash option or ½ of the lottery winner's "piece of the pie," could shrink the prize to an unviable amount.

Annuity vs. Cash Option Illustration

The most important factor in selecting a payment option is deciding which is right for you. While considering each payment method independently is beneficial, comparing the payment options together with small and large jackpots is also helpful.

For instance, if you win a $2 million jackpot and take the cash option you would receive approximately $1.12 million, the principal. After 25% in federal income tax and let's say 6% in state income taxes is withheld, you would take home a lump-sum check of $772,800.

If the annuity option is selected, you would receive an average payment of $80,000 (principal + interest) per year, for let's say 25 years. After taxes (6% in state and 25% in federal) are withheld, this average annual payment would be reduced to $55,200. But once the 25-year Treasury Bond is fully matured, the lottery winner would have taken home $1,380,000. Smaller jackpot winners often find that $55,200 per year for 25 years via the annuity option provides them with more long-term wealth and security.

For larger jackpots, the cash option may be less cumbersome. For example, if you win a $314.9 million lottery, such as Jack Whittaker of West Virginia, and take the lump-sum payment of $170.5 million, or $117.6 million after taxes, it may not matter since the net-prize amount is more than most could spend in a lifetime. The annuity option, 30 average annual payments of $10.49 million minus taxes, is still more profitable, but not nearly as critical to financial security.

Immediate Banking Needs

Since locating and hiring a quality Private Financial Manager is time consuming, many lottery winners temporarily deposit their winnings safely into their personal checking account. This is not necessarily the right thing to do.

First, the lottery winner should verify that the banking institution is a member of the Federal Deposit Insurance Corporation (FDIC). Deposits made in amounts up to $100,000 in banks or credit unions which are FDIC members are insured by the federal government. While the lottery winner may actually qualify for more than $100,000 coverage at a single bank, this requires that the winnings be placed in different accounts, such as separate accounts for spouses, joint accounts and retirement accounts.

Since you cannot simply deposit millions of dollars into the run-of-the-mill checking account, you will need to consult your bank about the special accounts necessary to hold your millions. Many lottery winners prefer to set-up accounts at two or more financial institutions so the funds are better insured.

In addition to interest-bearing checking and savings accounts, many lottery winners purchase short-term CDs (Certificate of Deposit) to protect their money. The 90 or 180 day CD should provide the lottery winner with enough time to hire the Private Financial Manager (see Human Resource Department).

The short-term goal is to protect the winnings without placing any long-term restrictions on the money until your Private Financial Manager has been retained and a sound financial plan has been devised. Remember, there is no rush!

7 Tax Department

Avoiding Taxes

Lottery winners may be lucky, but not even the Great Houdini could escape paying taxes. As they say, "It's the law," and just like everyone else, lottery winners must abide by the law. To assure that taxes are paid, lottery agencies are required to report all winnings of $599 or more to the IRS and state revenue departments. And to add insult to injury, the IRS's collection resources are without a doubt some of the most powerful and aggressive in the world.

The jackpot winner should keep in mind that by winning a multimillion-dollar prize, a red flag might be raised by the IRS and state revenue departments. Failure to follow the IRS's strict policies could jeopardize your lottery winnings.

A common and costly mistake made by individuals who inherit or win large sums of money is the failure to plan for future tax liabilities. Using the services of a Private Financial Manager (PFM^{CPA}) is the best way to ensure that your tax responsibilities are met. In addition to making sure the necessary tax forms are filed, the PFM ^{CPA} can help you understand changes in your filing status as well as actual tax responsibility (see Human Resource Department).

Another blunder made by people with wealth is to place too much trust in prestigious financial and accounting firms (remember Enron?). Despite the quality reputations that follow the big name firms, lottery winners need to be careful when buying into any tax shelter or other tax-reducing plan that sounds too good to be true.

Remember that in the majority of cases it is the client / taxpayer who suffers the consequences of tax fraud and not the white-collar criminal who designed the plan, marketed it and sold it. The lottery-winner may not be able to escape paying taxes, but at least he/she can avoid the stringent fines and penalties associated with rogue accounting practices, tax shelter scams and fraudulent tax filing.

Federal Taxes

It is the mission of the IRS to "...provide America's taxpayers top quality service by helping them understand and meet their tax responsibilities and by applying the tax law with integrity and fairness to all."[49] Since the reform of the Internal Revenue Service in 1998, you will find that the policies and employees of the agency are significantly more considerate and helpful than in the past.

According to the IRS, lottery winnings are considered ordinary income and thus susceptible to the federal income tax. In accordance with the Jobs & Growth Reconciliation Act of 2003, lottery winners have to pay 25% of their winnings in federal income taxes for prize payments in excess of $5,000 (Public Law 108-27).

Also, the amount of taxes withheld by the lottery agency may or may not cover the amount of taxes owed, so it is important to plan accordingly. The lottery winner's filing status will ultimately affect what is owed to the federal government.

IRS Tax Forms

All lottery winners will receive an IRS Form W-2G, Certain Gambling Winnings, in January of each year following the disbursement of prize winnings. This document will report the total prize payment received and the required federal income tax withholding amount for the previous tax year. The total amount printed in Box 1 of the W-2G Form will need to be reported on the "Other Income" line of your Form 1040.

The tax liability for group prize payments can often be divided between group members. You must complete the Internal Revenue Service's Form 5754 if you receive lottery winnings either for someone else or as a member of a group of winners on the same winning ticket. The PFM can assist you with meeting the strict deadlines of when and where IRS Form 5754 must be submitted.

Furthermore, lottery pools may also need a Federal Employer Identification Number (FEIN) to split tax responsibilities. Simply submit an IRS Form SS-4 to apply for an FEIN. All tax forms can be ordered through the Internal Revenue Service's website (www.irs.gov) or by calling 800-829-3676.

State Taxes

States may exempt lottery tickets from a sales tax, but most are rigorous about collecting income taxes on grand prizes. Depending on the state or province, the lottery winner will be required to pay a percentage (less than 10%) of the jackpot in state income taxes.

Similar to federal income tax withholdings, lottery winners should keep in mind that the amount initially withheld may or may not sufficiently meet the state income tax burden. During the claims process the lottery agency will only estimate the state income tax owed and will leave the ultimate responsibility in the hands of the jackpot winner. The reason for this is that the individual filing status of the lottery winner(s) is used to calculate the exact amount of tax owed.

Depending on where the claimant(s) lives and the state where the ticket was purchased, state income taxes may or may not be imposed on lottery winnings. Residents of some lotto-states, such as Florida, Texas, and Wyoming do not have to pay income taxes.

In some cases, the out-of-state lottery winner may have to pay a partial income tax in the state where the ticket was purchased as well as their resident state. But in other jurisdictions, the out-of-state lottery winner only has to pay income taxes if she holds residence in the state on a part-time basis. Most often lottery winners only pay state income taxes in their resident state.

Local Taxes

As "creatures of the State," local governments are rarely allowed to withhold income taxes from lottery winnings. Generally, local governments rely on such revenue sources as user fees, licenses and property taxes to finance community services.

Taxes Withheld on Non-U.S. Citizens

Lottery winners who are not U.S. citizens, do not have a social security number, or do not have a federal identification number will have to pay a premium in income taxes. The "special income tax" for non-U.S. citizens usually ranges from 1 to 3 percent for state income taxes.

The federal income tax rate for non-U.S. citizens is 3% above that which citizens pay. In accordance with the Jobs & Growth Reconciliation Act of 2003, lottery winners without a social security or federal identification number are required to pay 28% (instead of 25%), of their winnings in federal income taxes.

In addition to paying a premium in incomes taxes, the lottery winner who is an illegal alien in the United States is usually deported. This has happened in all known cases of lottery winners who were in the U.S. illegally.

Double Tax Scenario

The annuity-opted lottery winner may have to pay taxes on both the first and second year prize installments during a single filing. For this to occur, the lottery winner would have to claim their jackpot in late December of one year and receive the first and second prize payment in the following year. While this can only happen under the initial circumstance of the first and second prize installment, the lottery winner in this situation should prepare for the double income tax scenario.

Accounts Payable Department

Liens & Levies

Creditors and government entities have a legal right to file a lien or levy against lottery winners in an effort to collect payment on debt(s). While the lien may only attach itself to the lottery winner's home, the levy can be attached to wages, financial accounts and, yes, lottery prize installments.

A levy on lottery winnings is considered continuous. That is, until the debt is released or the tax is paid in full, it will continue to attach itself to future prize payments. The amount of the debt is subtracted from the net amount of the prize payment(s) until the debt is paid in full.

Back-Taxes

As one of life's few guarantees, you can count on the IRS and/or state revenue departments to collect any back-taxes you may owe. There are several instances of lottery winners going to claim their winnings only to find their prize reduced substantially by the deduction of back-taxes. During the claims process, lottery agencies are required to investigate whether or not you owe the government(s) any money.

It works like this. The Internal Revenue Service puts taxpayers who owe the IRS money into the State Income Tax Levy Program (SITLP). This is in addition to a Notice of Federal Tax Lien they will record in the county where the lottery winner resides.

During the claims process, the lottery agency will check to see if the claimant owes the state any back taxes. The SITLP red flags both state and federal income tax debts for prizes over $5,000.

Student Loans

Lottery winners with outstanding federal student loans should plan on having the debt withheld from their prize winnings. In the same manner as back-tax debts, student loans are red flagged during the claims process. The lottery winner with outstanding student-loan debts may be able to expedite the claims process by bringing their student loan account information with them to the lottery headquarters.

Bankruptcy

The purpose of bankruptcy is to provide businesses and individuals with an opportunity to reorganize financial debt without fear of retaliation from creditors. As part of the protection granted by the courts, all income, including lottery winnings, received after the bankruptcy filing cannot be touched by creditors. The lottery winner involved in bankruptcy proceedings should seek legal counsel prior to claiming their prize.

Social Security

Lottery winners who receive Social Security do not have to worry about their good fortune affecting what is rightfully theirs. The amount of benefit received from Social Security is determined by gross wages earned from employment and not personal income.

According to the Social Security Administration, they "use gross wages as the basis for Social Security credit and for determining whether benefits must be withheld because of earnings.... Non-work sources of income, such as: inheritance payments, pensions, income from investments, IRA distributions, interest, [lottery winnings] or other sources do not count as wages for the earnings test."[50]

Welfare Recipients

With the introduction of numerous welfare-to-work type programs, both state and federal, it has become more difficult for individuals who do not need financial help to receive welfare benefits. When the welfare recipient wins a lottery jackpot, he/she is required to inform their Social Services Counselor of the income. Not to do so voluntarily would most certainly constitute fraud.

Obviously, the winner of a multimillion-dollar lottery would cease to meet the need requirements necessary to receive welfare benefits and thus would no longer be eligible for them. Most welfare recipients turned lottery winner are only too happy to no longer need public assistance.

Child Support

Since the induction of federal and state Child Support Enforcement Programs and the National Electronic Child Support Resource System, the lottery winner who is delinquent in making child support payments may have to pay up during the claims process. One POWERBALL® winner learned this the hard way.

> A POWERBALL® winner was ordered to pay $880,000 to a fund for future child support. On July 22, 2000 a Kentucky man won a $65.4 million dollar jackpot. He chose the lump sum option and was to receive $34.1 million. Just as lottery officials were about to clear him to receive his money, the state was notified that the winner had been behind in child support since 1986 and owed $31,000. A judge then ordered the man to pay $880,000 into a fund for future support.[51]

Child support debt is a state-by-state issue that fluctuates greatly, depending on such variables as the host states' policies, the specific lottery game, the residency of the dependent(s), and the residence of the claimant. Some Lotteries only offset winnings if the back child-support debt is over a specific amount. For example, Rhode Island's "set off" provision for child support debt only applies to unpaid amounts in excess of $500.00.

Nevertheless, the Federal Office of Child Support Enforcement (OCSE), an entity of the U.S. Department of Health and Human Services, asserts that "Many (not all) State Child Support Enforcement Programs have the authority to intercept in-state lottery winnings of individuals owing a child support debt, child support arrearages, spousal support and child support cost in their state."[52]

The OCSE also maintains that many, but not all, Child Support Enforcement Programs can collect on multi-state lottery [game] winnings [e.g. POWERBALL®, [53] BIG GAME® [54], LOTTO SOUTH® [55]], but ONLY if the ticket is purchased in the same state that has the child support debt on their statewide child-support enforcement system AND the ticket is cashed in the same state.

Alimony

Can divorce be cost-prohibitive? According to the U.S. Census Bureau, divorce is a leading cause of single parent poverty[56]. Because of the financial impact, courts often require alimony, also known as spousal maintenance, to be paid from one spouse to the other. Alimony payments can be lump sum, temporary, permanent or purely for reimbursement.

The policies for determining the need and extent of alimony vary between jurisdictions. Such factors as duration of marriage, earning capacity of each spouse, age and medical condition, and other income (e.g. interest, dividends, lottery winnings) are considered relevant issues in alimony cases.

Just as any court-imposed debt, back-alimony may be withheld from lottery winnings during the claims process. It should not be ignored that alimony judgments can be revised under special circumstances. Lottery winners with spousal maintenance obligations or who are involved in alimony proceedings should consult their divorce attorney before claiming their jackpot.

Divorce

In contrast to the 2,187,000 couples that married last year in the United States, more than 83,000 filed for divorce (est. 2003).[57] With financial hardship as a leading cause for lingering marriages and divorce, it is easy to understand how winning a ton of money in a lottery could entice some couples to go their separate ways. Unlike the happily married couple that typically stays together after a jackpot win, dissatisfied spouses may see the financial windfall as a means to escape a bad relationship.

Like matches and gasoline, divorce and lottery winnings can be an explosive mixture. Such factors as the State's property scheme (common or community property law), jurisdictional authority, funds used to purchase the lottery ticket and the circumstances surrounding the marriage, can influence the division of lottery winnings during a divorce.

Lottery winners who are considering or involved in a marital separation or divorce should use extreme caution and expert legal advice before claiming a jackpot prize. Not to do so could easily turn your once-in-a-lifetime good fortune into a rest-of-your-life regret. The seriousness and complexity of divorce and the division of lottery winnings can be illustrated with a few examples.

A 65-year-old man of Appleton, Wisconsin was convicted of perjury after trying to conceal $75,000 in lottery winnings from his ex-wife. Despite the fact that his lottery pool won the $250,000 Supercash® jackpot a month after the divorce was filed, the judge found him guilty of lying under oath when he failed to disclose the income during court proceedings.[58] The man was sentenced to six months in jail and three years probation.

In addition to losing your freedom, failing to disclose lottery winnings during divorce proceedings may also mean that you lose the money. One woman got a first-hand look at California's community property laws.

Nearly two years after a hurried divorce, the California State Lottery Commission confirmed Thomas Rossi's suspicion that his ex-wife, Denise, had won a lottery jackpot and kept it a secret.

> The jackpot prize was $6,680,000, and Denise's share was $1,336,000, to be paid in 20 equal annual installments of $66,800 less taxes, from 1996 through 2015. ... In early January 1997, Denise filed a petition for dissolution of marriage in the Los Angles Superior Court. She never told Thomas about the lottery jackpot. She used her mother's address to receive checks and other information from the California Lottery so that her husband Thomas would not learn of the windfall.[59]

In May of 1999, after confirming that Denise had "hit the jackpot" 11 days before demanding an immediate divorce, Mr. Rossi brought an action of fraud, failure to disclose (concealment), breach of fiduciary duty, and malice against his former wife of 25 years.

Mrs. Rossi argued that her lottery winnings were separate property gifted to her from co-workers who had formed a lottery pool, but Superior Court Judge Richard Denner thought otherwise. In his ruling, he found that she had violated state disclosure laws and determined that she acted out of fraud or malice. Denise was ordered to give 100% of her lottery winnings to her ex-husband. She appealed the decision but lost.

While courts are unilaterally strict about full disclosure of assets during divorce proceedings, their views on when a marriage is officially over can vary. Some require the official decree of divorce to be filed with the court while others may consider the time in which the couple begins living "separate and apart". According to a CDC, National Center for Health Statistics report,

> Marriages that end do not always end in divorce; many end in separation and do not go through the divorce process.[60]

A Maryland man won a lottery jackpot in excess of a million dollars and thought it was his. After being legally separated for nearly two years, Mr. Alston's ex-wife retracted her initial petition for divorce and filed a second complaint several months later seeking a share of the prize money. Citing his infidelity, Mrs. Alston was granted 50% of his lottery winnings from the trial court.

After much debate, the Court of Appeals reversed the decision noting that "how and when specific marital property" was acquired and the contribution made by each party should be considered. The Alston court stated that:

> Where one party, wholly through his or her own efforts, and without any direct or indirect contribution by the other, acquires a specific item of marital property after the parties have separated and after the marital family has, as a practical matter, ceased to exist, a monetary award representing an equal division of that particular property would not ordinarily be consonant with the history and purpose of the statute.[61]

After deciding that there was "no evidence which would justify awarding any portion of the annuity to Mrs. Alston," the Court of Appeals reversed the lower court's ruling that had given her 50% of the prize. Although Mr. Alston was able to keep 100% of his winnings, the case was remanded back to the trial court to revisit the issue of alimony.[62]

The common position of the courts is that once a divorce is finalized, neither spouse is required to further share debt or income. Prior to the final dissolution of the marriage, however, all debt and income, such as lottery winnings, may be considered mutual property. Lottery winners who are considering divorce, who are separated, or who are engaged in divorce proceedings should consult their divorce attorney before claiming the jackpot.

8 Public Relations Department

The Lottery Winner's 15 Minutes of Fame

Chasing fame may be a part of the American dream, but is it for everyone? From popular reality television shows to waving frantically behind the local newscaster, many Americans seem to be infatuated with what one pop culture expert calls "pure slobbering attention." "Humans have an almost pathological behavioral characteristic that makes them scream out 'Look at me!'" says Robert Thompson, director of the Center for the Study of Popular Television and a professor at Syracuse University.[63]

But, in addition to chasing financial dreams, are lottery winners necessarily looking for fame too? For the lottery winner who answers, "Yes!" there will be plenty of opportunities for media attention and local popularity contests. Most lottery-winners however, exhibit a preference to return to a more normal private life without the "slobbering attention."

The Interview Option

If the lottery agency feels that your experience is newsworthy, they will invite you to participate in a press conference. Such stories as rags-to-riches, unique situations, exciting circumstances and large jackpots are usually considered newsworthy and marketable to the public. Local community media outlets are more likely to interview smaller jackpot winners.

Deciding whether or not to take part in the press conference is a personal decision, which only the lottery winner(s) can make. This *optional* interview is scheduled during the claims process and depending on the host agency, will take place anywhere from 1 to 72 hours after the winning ticket's authenticity has been verified.

Of course, there are several advantages and disadvantages to giving a press conference. One benefit is that it gives the lottery winner the opportunity to receive his/her 15 minutes of fame. And it is believed that participating in the press conference enhances the lottery winning experience.

One disadvantage to the press conference is the personal publicity. Many lottery winners are not comfortable with being the center of public attention. It cannot be ignored that whatever is said, done or communicated during the interview will be heard, read, seen and judged by the viewing public.

The amount of media attention is directly related to the size of the jackpot and the circumstances surrounding the winner(s). An interesting back-story will also drive media attention. Jack Whittaker, the West Virginian who won the largest undivided jackpot in U.S. history (2002), learned this the hard way.

> Since his $314.9 million Powerball® win, the charitable businessman with a devotion to his family, church and community has been the center of numerous attention-getting back-stories. From having over half-a-million dollars stolen to being arrested for drunk driving to the unrelated death of his 18-year old granddaughter, Mr. Whittaker's troubles have continued to make national headlines.

Mr. Whittaker's own words, "If I had it to do over, I'd be more secluded about it" shows his remorse for engaging the spotlight. In addition to public embarrassment, the Whittaker family has also been the target of various wrongdoings and civil lawsuits.

Lottery winners should be aware that the press conference has the potential to increase personal risk. By putting a face with a name, the lottery winner automatically becomes more recognizable and susceptible to wrong doings. Covered in the Security Department, the lottery winner should take all necessary safety and privacy precautions before giving the press conference.

Nevertheless, declining the press conference may not keep the lottery-winner from "slobbering attention."[64] Some publicity experts believe that the press conference is an excellent opportunity for jackpot-winners to satisfy public curiosity and divert financial decisions to their advisors. By declining, the lottery-winner may cause more interest and curiosity than by simply coming out and announcing his/her happiness and gratitude for the financial windfall.

The Lottery Winner's Press Conference

The lottery winners' press conference is an important event and should be taken seriously. As the recipient of a prize generated in a public-lottery, the jackpot winner needs to recognize his/her social situation and accept the reward with grace and dignity. Planning and preparation is the best way to ensure grace and avoid public embarrassment during the press conference.

When people remember the most important events in their lives, they want to do so with pride and not embarrassment or regret. For instance, lottery winners often feel more comfortable if they are dressed appropriately for the interview. No one wants to remember the momentous occasion wearing a worn-out T-shirt or a wrinkled suit. The following list of interview tips was designed to help lottery winners give an effective and professional press conference.

Interview Tips

1. Dress professionally or in your "Sunday best."
2. Assume cameras and microphones are recording from the moment you enter the Press Hall until the instant you exit the room. Every thing you say, do and gesture may be quoted or televised by the news media.
3. Use pleasant facial expressions & control emotions.
4. Do not use profanity and avoid using slang.
5. Keep answers short, responsive and to the point.
6. Avoid naming any charity or cause to which you are considering a donation.
7. Do not make derogatory or slanderous statements.
8. Project your voice clearly and loudly enough for everyone in the Press Hall to hear you.
9. Be polite and helpful to the press; they will be the ones talking about you!
10. Be sure to hold and display promotional checks in front of you correctly.

Lottery Promotional Checks

Lottery agencies often present the claimant(s) with a promotional lottery check during the press conference. Promotional checks are approximately 40 inches in width, 21 inches in height, and very light in weight. To be exhibited by the jackpot winner, the commemorative check should be held at waist level and in plain view of the audience.

As a marketing tool for the lottery game, the cardboard display also serves as a souvenir for the claimant. While it may appear to be an actual check with all the proper signatures, it is non-negotiable and *cannot be cashed.*

Sample Interview Questions

Before the interview, the lottery winner should anticipate the questions that are typically asked and then rehearse their answers.

Even experienced public speakers rehearse in front of a mirror or familiar audience before going public with their message. This way, you can get a feeling for what you will say, how you will say it and what non-verbal gestures are appropriate for the occasion. The lottery winner who prepares and rehearses for the interview will be able to look back on the occasion with pride rather than embarrassment.

The lottery-winner's interview usually begins with specific yes/no questions and concludes with open-ended inquiries. Listed below is a series of frequently asked questions that are commonly found in the press conference:

1. How long have you played the specific lottery game?

2. Will you ever play the lottery again?
3. Where did you purchase the winning ticket and under what circumstances?
4. To what do you attribute your winning the lottery?
5. How did you react when you found out you had a winning jackpot ticket?
6. Are you employed, how long have you worked there, and do you plan on quitting?
7. Do you plan on sharing any of your winnings with family and/or friends?
8. Are there any specific charities to which you plan to give?
9. What do you plan to do with your lottery winnings?
10. How will winning the lottery change your life?

Safety Issues for the Interviewee

Lottery winners should not divulge any information during the interview that could jeopardize personal safety. Such things as personal contact information, travel plans, personal affiliations or the identity of family and friends should not be exposed to the media. Taking such safety precautions can help deter criminals from targeting you, your property and/or your family and friends.

Legal Issues for the Interviewee

Typically a low-pressure and friendly interview, the press conference is still an occasion that must be taken seriously. The interviewee should be cautious and avoid making statements that could have legal consequences. It would be tragic to say the wrong thing and have to spend your honeymoon in court, making unrealistic contributions, or even worse, in jail.

Especially during the press conference, the lottery winner should refrain from making any defamatory/slanderous statements, which are considered both criminal and personal tort violations. Statements about public figures, organizations, employers, adversaries and groups (e.g., political, religious, national origins, genders) should not be voiced. Instead, only a rosy worldview should be expressed.

Lottery winners should also avoid naming any specific person or organization to which he/she *plans* on making a donation. Similarly, declaring specific amounts of contributions to be made is a bad idea. Such public statements could be considered oral contracts and thus legally binding.

It is also important to recognize that federal law authorizes the government to confiscate lottery winnings under special circumstances. For this reason, jackpot winners should not make any statement, regardless of sincerity or context, which could imply their involvement in a crime or wrongdoing. A $12 million Texas Lottery winner got a first-hand look at the long-arm of the law.

According to a June 4, 2003, Immediate Release from the U.S. Department of Justice, U.S. Attorney's Office of the Southern District of Texas:

> … Jose Betancourt, 52, a resident alien from Mexico residing in Brownsville, Texas, [was found] guilty of conspiracy and two counts of possession with intent to distribute cocaine… [The report stated that] following the return of the guilty verdicts, the trial continued on the

government's claim to forfeit monies Betancourt derived from his drug trafficking to include lottery winnings. In this regard, the jury heard testimony about Betancourt having won the Texas Lottery worth $12 million in December 2002.

On January 14th, after lottery officials verified his winning ticket, approximately $5.5 million, representing the cash out proceeds minus an amount withheld for federal income taxes, was deposited into Betancourt's bank account. Two days later, Betancourt delivered the cocaine that led to his arrest and Friday's convictions.

Federal law authorizes the government to seek the forfeit of all property and proceeds obtained from drug trafficking and any monies or other property obtained with those proceeds… With the jury's second verdict, the court ordered Betancourt to forfeit his interest in the more than $5.5 million in lottery winnings and an additional $76,000, which the jury found constituted the proceeds of his drug trafficking activity.[65]

Giving to Family and Friends

While cultures differ in the practice of gift giving, the fact that many lottery winners share their winnings with family and friends is endearing. Jackpot winners often feel that sharing their wealth enhances the winning experience.

But when the lottery winner *chooses* to share his/her winnings, the Private Financial Manager (PFM) should be consulted first. The PFM will incorporate the gifts into your financial plan while at the same time minimizing any loss and/or tax liability. Remember that the tax burden is most often the responsibility of the lottery winner (the gifter).

Such tools as the Federal Unified Gift and Estate Tax Credit can help the lottery winner minimize the gift tax. Did you know that you and your spouse, given that he/she is a U.S. citizen, can give up to $22,000 each year to as many people you choose tax-free?

The PFM may be able to help you minimize gift taxes, but only you can make fair and objective decisions regarding how you share your winnings. The flip side to the effects of money is its ability to cause harm, resentment, and dissension among families and friends.

- **Personal Relationships and Gifting**

Because of jealousy, expectations, or a sense of entitlement, financial windfalls often damage personal relationships. The majority of lottery winners consider siblings to be the most difficult to satisfy, but it is not unheard of for children, parents, friends and even co-workers to aggressively solicit gifts.

While being taken advantage of is a familiar complaint among lottery winners, most consider the ability to help family and friends as a positive. The goal is to be fair and considerate of personal relationships.

When Mr. and Mrs. James Lewis won a $22.9 million POWERBALL® jackpot in August of 2000, they immediately recognized the potential hazards of their good fortune and were careful to whom, how and when they presented their gifts.[66] According to the conscientious couple, "We've got some very serious work to do. It's so much money, if we're not careful, this could really hurt a family."[67]

If the lottery winner chooses to gift family members or friends, it should not be overlooked that the amount of gift-giving can be considered a valid measurement of the importance placed on each individual relationship. For this reason, lottery winners should use tact, fairness and objectivity when giving gifts.

- **Hierarchy-Gifting Method**

The *hierarchy-gifting method* allocates gifts from the closest of blood kin to the outermost relationships. Since family hierarchies are organized differently between cultures and family structures, the lottery winner will have to apply his/her own objectivity and beliefs to the hierarchy-gifting method.

It works like this. Let's pretend the lottery winner is a single father with two adult children, married and living parents, two siblings, and two lifelong friends.

With a lump-sum payment minus applicable taxes that amounts to $10 million, the single parent may want to give 9% to each child, 5% to his married parents, 3% to *each* sibling, and 1% to each lifelong friend. After gifting 31%, or $3.1 million to family and friends, the lottery winner is able to enjoy his $6.9 million net holdings without fear of leaving anyone out, creating resentment or showing favoritism.

Giving to Charities

The belief that people who give to charities are egoists and bargaining for honor or social promotion may be true for some, but the actions of "typical" lottery winners contradict this stereotype.

Unlike public figures or organizations, lottery winners rarely schedule press conferences or news releases to boast about their generosity. In fact, lottery winners are more often heard discussing the personal stimulation and positive emotional feelings regarding their contribution rather than the size of donation or the trendy cause. According to Ileana Rodriguez, the February 2003 LOTTO SOUTH® jackpot winner, "It feels good to give."[68]

While the personal gratification is significant, so too is the number of laws and tax codes that apply to making charitable donations. For instance, the non-profit organization must have a 501(c) (3) tax rating with the IRS in order for your donation to be a "write off". Remember that the goal is for your heart and your wallet to be in the right place!

Failure to prepare for the actual tax burden associated with charitable gifting is a common and costly mistake among the suddenly wealthy. Despite the tax deduction earned from contributing to a qualified charity, the benefit you receive will not equal the full amount of the gift. So, before committing (publicly or privately) to any non-profit organization, you should consult your Private Financial Manager (PFM) and be prepared to pay the remaining tax.

9 Privacy Department

The Lottery Winner's Right to Privacy

Privacy is a thing of the past. Americans now live in a society with background history databases, government Echelon Dictionary systems that record attention-getting content from telephone conversations, and companies that specialize in collecting and selling information about you. According to one political expert, "The intrusion is shadowed by regulations that provide an appearance of homeland security and privacy from commercial nuisances."

Since remaining anonymous isn't an option, most lottery winners take action to combat commercial nuisances. In doing so, the lottery winner will need to use various privacy controls and security measures.

Remaining Anonymous

Lottery winners often wish to remain anonymous for a variety of reasons. Some wish to stay anonymous to protect their privacy while the non-U.S. citizen may wish to avoid deportation. Regardless of the reason, certain information about every jackpot winner is released to the public.

State and province laws not only direct the release of the lottery winner's identity, the Freedom of Information Act and Internal Revenue Service policies usually prohibit lottery agencies from concealing information regarding the use or disbursement of lottery funds. The State of Delaware is the only jurisdiction that allows lottery winners to remain anonymous.

In other instances, the lottery winner's name(s), the game played, and the name and location of the retailer who sold the winning ticket is considered public information. Additionally, the gross and net amounts of prize payments are public domain. In States such as New York, lottery winners' who win $1 million or more must allow their photograph to be disclosed to the public.

Information such as telephone numbers and addresses are not disclosed to the public. As a matter of candor, the release of winner information serves as a check-and-balance to assure other players that lottery proceeds are in fact paid to prizewinners.

Privacy Controls

Lottery winners can protect their privacy by controlling commercial nuisances. Commercial nuisances include beggars, cold-call investors, salespeople, telemarketers and any source that aggressively solicits business, products or causes.

Jackpot winners have an array of options when it comes to protecting their privacy. From employing a telephone answering service to changing contact information to installing privacy fences, there are numerous ways to protect your privacy.

First, lottery winners should refer all legal and business matters to their financial advisors- even if they're imaginary. Using the press conference as a sounding board and deterrent is an excellent privacy control. A simple statement made during the press conference indicating that all financial decisions will be made in strict consultation with your advisors can be extremely effective. Not only does this lessen the appearance of your decision-making authority, but it also emphasizes that all financial decisions will be highly scrutinized.

Another privacy control is the use of a Post Office Box for all sales pitches and business proposals. Lottery winners should maintain that only proposals received through their P.O. Box will be considered. Those received by any other means will be discarded unopened. It should be pointed out that your advisors will contact them *if* the charity, program or proposal is chosen. This privacy control will reduce bogus offers and highlight those worthy of your attention.

Another strategy used by the financially wealthy is to have the Private Financial Manager or Security Consultant protect his/her paper trail. Information such as credit reports, insurance records, credit card balances, Social Security status, criminal and driving records, employment and educational histories, and names of lottery winners are some of the most highly sought after items in the marketplace. Protecting such information from being sold and distributed is an important privacy control among the financially affluent.

As the tool-of-choice for most commercial pests, the telephone is an obvious personal gateway that will need to be protected. By simply contacting your telephone company and paying a small monthly fee, you can have your telephone number(s) unlisted. In most cases, lottery winners acquire a new unlisted telephone number altogether.

Other contact numbers, such as fax, cellular and E-mail addresses, may also need to be safeguarded. But for these privacy controls to be effective it is important for *everyone* with your contact information to respect the need for confidentiality.

Another personal gateway that is easily invaded is the curbside mailbox. Lottery winners who wish to combat the increase in junk mail, telemarketers, pre-approved credit offers and direct mailings can register with a variety of services. Table 9.1 lists some of the registry services and the types of nuisance from which they can protect the lottery winner.

TABLE 9.1

Type of Nuisance	Service Name	Contact Information
Telemarketers	National Do Not Call Registry	(888) 382-1222 www.donotcall.com
Telemarketers	Direct Marketing Association (D.M.A)	P.O. Box 9014 Farmingdale, NY 11735 www.dmaconsumers.org
Direct Mailings	Direct Marketing Preference Service Manager	1120 Ave. of Americas New York, NY 10036 www.the-dma.org
Direct Mail & Telemarketing	D.M.A. (State Do-Not-Call List)	www.the-dma.org/government/donotcalllists.shtml
Pre-Approved Credit & Junk Mail	Credit Reporting Industry	1-888-5-OPTOUT (888) 567-8688
	Pre-screen Opt-Out	Removes Name from four Credit Agencies

Security Department

Security Needs Analysis

In many ways, privacy controls and security measures go hand-in-hand. A fenced property line not only prevents beggars from ringing your doorbell, but it also discourages would-be criminals from trespassing.

Lottery winners should use a security system that takes their specific needs into account. The size of the lottery jackpot and the amount of public interest should be considered when measuring the level security that is needed.

While many jackpot winners feel comfortable with basic home security systems, it should not be overlooked that the financially affluent are more likely to be the target of criminal acts. For this reason, people with wealth often seek advice from professional security consultants to enhance their safety at home, in transit and in their person.

Professional Security Consultants

Professional security consultants and services come in an array of shapes and sizes, which can make selecting the provider a difficult task. There are numerous issues to consider when hiring professionals to provide security for you and your family.

Financially wealthy people usually prefer security consultants that are independent and commission-free from businesses that provide system services, products or components. This is important for the lottery winner who wants a security system tailored to his/her needs without bias to any particular product.

The initial selection criteria should include the qualifications and training of security providers and their employees. Formal education, background, credentials, and experience in providing security to the financially affluent are good pre-employment selection criteria. References are a must, and do your homework by contacting each one scrupulously.

The primary function of the independent security consultant is to analyze the needs of the individual(s) and design a security system and procedure protocol that maximizes safety and minimizes threat. To do this, the consultant will perform some version of a security needs analysis or risk assessment that correlates with the client's needs and/or wants. Once the hardware and procedures are agreed upon, the consultant will use qualified internal personnel or bonded contractors to install the systems and/or provide personal security services.

Home Security

Designing, installing and maintaining home security systems are often the security consultant's primary objective. Providing estate and home security is important because of the psychological need to feel safe and secure in our personal living quarters. From fire and burglar alarms with satellite backup to access controlled security gates and strategic lighting designs, the professional security consultant has many tools and deterrents to keep your home safe.

Transportation Security

Another goal of security consultants is to maximize safety and minimize threats for the client while in transit. Transportation security is important because of the increase in vulnerability that comes with being in continuously changing environments. Security consultants use such tools as satellite-tracking systems, alternative-route planning, and protective driving measures to reduce safety risks while in transit.

Personal Security

Security services can also provide the client with physical personal security. While this type of security is critical for high profile clients, it is not uncommon for people with wealth to employ personal bodyguards or escorts. We already know that many lottery agencies provide the claimant(s) with a personal security guard for the claims process, but it is not unheard of for jackpot winners to be escorted by their own.

Bodyguards come in an array of forms: Armed or Unarmed, Uniformed or Plain Clothes, Male or Female. They can also be hired on a full-time, part-time or special event basis.

Securing the Winning Lottery Ticket

Upon realizing that you have a winning number set, it is of the utmost importance to cautiously secure the lottery ticket. Just as cash is a bearer instrument, so too is a lottery ticket until it is signed. In other words, if you do not sign the back of the ticket and you lose it, someone else could legally claim you jackpot. For this reason, it is recommended that lottery tickets be filled out and signed when purchased.

Nevertheless, immediately after the winning set of numbers is discovered, the lottery should confirm that the backside of the ticket is completed and signed. If you have not filled-out and signed the ticket, you should do so *immediately*. This will certify that you are the rightful owner of the lottery ticket.

KEEP Dry

DO NOT IRON

AVOID HEAT

KEEP SAFE

It is also a good idea to photocopy (front and back) the ticket on a GLASS-TOP copying machine so as to alleviate the need to handle the actual ticket. The photocopies can be used for *informal* representation of ownership, for winning-number confirmation, and for exhibition purposes.

Until you are prepared and ready for the claims process, the lottery ticket should be secured under lock-and-key, combination, and/or personal monitoring. Adequate home safes usually cost only a few hundred dollars and can be purchased at many local retail and hardware stores. Fireproof safes and safety deposit boxes are the most practical storage devices to secure the winning lottery ticket.

Cautious lottery winners will keep the winning ticket on their person whenever in transit. Lottery agency officials have been presented with winnings tickets from a variety of concealed locations, including freezer bags, shoes, and undergarments. In the event you are mugged, carjacked, or if your luggage is lost, at least your ticket to a life of luxury will not be forsaken.

Lottery Drawing Security

How secure are lottery drawings? Without a doubt lottery drawings are some of the most secure and highly scrutinized events in modern-day society. From an array of agency policies to an assortment of checks-and-balances, lottery drawings are meticulously safeguarded from corruption.

To ensure public trust and confidence, lottery agencies are proactive in preventing fraud. For instance, lottery officials, family members who reside in the same residence, ticket vendors, and contractors are not allowed to participate in lottery games.

All lotteries use some combination of security procedures to guarantee that lottery numbers are selected at random and that drawings are not rigged. While states and provinces vary in how security is applied to drawings, policies and formal procedures are *always* followed to guarantee public trust. For example, security protocols often include the following:

- Two lottery officials arrive 3 hours before the drawing.
- At least one external auditor arrives 3 hours before the drawing.
- Machines and ball sets are tested, checked and chosen at random.
- Drawing rehearsals are conducted with television crews and the drawing host.
- Machines and ball sets are locked in a secure room prior to and after a drawing.
- Lottery officials, an external auditor, the television crew and host, and the viewing public are present to witness the actual lottery drawing.

10 Human Resource Department

The Key to Avoiding Lotto-Winner Bankruptcy

Picking the winning set of numbers may be the hard part, but holding onto your lottery purse is no easy task. No matter how large the jackpot is that you win, if your winnings are not managed properly, you stand to lose it all.

For one reason or another, people who inherit a "*fool's treasure*" are notorious for falling victim to investment scams, incompetent advice or the stringent policies of the Internal Revenue Service. They get to witness their riches slip between their fingers. As the cliché says, the only thing worse than never having money is to have money and then lose it. Don't let this happen to you!

You have taken the first step toward being successful in your quest to STAY WEALTHY. You purchased this book. The second step is to do as the financially affluent do-- hire *true professionals* who are trained and experienced in protecting large sums of wealth.

When James and Sharon Lewis, MN, won their $22.9 million POWERBALL® jackpot, they knew they had "some very serious work to do." According to Lewis, he "assembled a team of investment counselors, accountants and lawyers to advise his family on how to take the money, and what to do with it."[69]

The financially affluent understand that staying wealthy is as much about their ability to recognize their own lack of financial expertise, as it is their responsibility to hire quality professionals who are proficient in managing their complex needs. This is not to say that you have to become a financial expert and understand all the details and technical language, but you must take absolute control over whose advice you accept and who is allowed to represent you.

According to one lottery winner, "… [I] can't fully retire because I have to manage my winnings." Yes, while managing your lottery winnings will become a routine activity, it will also be something you can enjoy, provided that you employ individuals who are personally compatible and professionally competent.

Your lack of experience in financial management, investment and asset protection is in no way different from America's wealthiest, who, by the way, never admit to being financially savvy. What the financially affluent do admit, however, is that their wealth was acquired through various other means and they do not have the technical expertise necessary to place, invest and protect large sums of money.

So whether you've just won $5 million or $500 million, your best chance to avoid financial pitfalls or even bankruptcy is to employ *true professionals* who can help you stay wealthy. Make sure that your once-in-a-lifetime good fortune is a rest-of-your-life benefit.

Professionals for Lottery Winners

Have you ever stayed up late watching television? If you have, then you have probably seen the scores of get-rich schemes that are being sold. Fortunately, most of us realize that the majority of people behind these schemes are scam artists. What viewers may not realize is that it is even easier to get scammed by professionals.

So, how do you distinguish between the scam artist and the professional? The scam artist is often recognizable because he /she is unlicensed and does not have a formal education in the profession. While all states require attorneys and certified public accountants to be licensed, it takes no license to call oneself an advisor. Beware of these "Barber Shop Consultants."

Distinguishing between the junior professional and the true professional is more difficult because both have similar qualifications, services, and official sounding titles. To differentiate between the two, the financially affluent often use reputation and the size and wealth of the advisors' clientele

For the purposes of this reading, the *true professional* is the licensed attorney and/or accountant with an employment history that includes recognizable and reputable firms. He/she will also have at least a decade of verifiable experience in managing the affairs of a small yet wealthy clientele. The true professional will be more difficult to locate because they tend to rely more on word-of-mouth than advertisement or self-promotion.

- **Junior Professionals**

Lottery winners should not use the inexperienced professional-- the junior professional. The 29-year-old Investment Broker with 5 years of experience may adhere to the profession's standards and be competent enough to handle the investments of many, but he is not yet qualified to manage *your* millions. It takes years, if not decades, of experience in the finance, accounting and legal professions to acquire the skills and abilities necessary to manage the affairs of the financially affluent.

Junior professionals are more visible as they are found on the front-line of solicitations, cold-calls, and self-promotion. With little or no experience, these professionals are often employed by large and sometimes reputable firms to solicit the business of the average investor.

- **Family Professionals**

Family members and friends with experience in investing, accounting or law are often excellent sources of information and reference, but with the high stakes that are involved, they should NOT be used to manage your affairs. It is in everyone's best interest to employee only the services of unbiased professionals with client / counsel boundaries. While family and friend professionals are priceless interim resources, using them permanently is a deadly trap that you want to avoid.

Professional Qualifications

As a first-time shopper, the lottery winner needs to be insistently careful in whom he/she chooses as their Private Financial Manager (PFM). Not only are there numerous official-sounding titles that can be misleading, but there are also a countless number of fancy sales presentations and financial reports that are used to sell professional services. The lottery winner should initially examine the professionals' licenses and qualifications without placing too much emphasis on titles.

The best PFM will not only hold the Attorney at Law and CPA designation, but he/she will also carry a variety of other qualifications that enhance their professional standing.

- **Private Financial Managers**

The financially affluent often select the Private Financial Manager (PFM) who is skilled, experienced, and licensed in various professional areas. It is easier to work with a single PFM who is licensed to manage your legal affairs, tax filings, and financial planning rather than three separate individuals.

The suitable PFM, also known as a Private Wealth Manager (PWM), will be the individual who can successfully manage the lottery winner's affairs. He/she will have an excellent grasp of investment tools, accounting and tax practices, estate planning and law.

He/she should also be one with whom you can develop a supportive and trusting rapport. As the employer of your advisor, it is important that a quality long-term relationship can be developed and maintained. It is not unusual for the elite client to confide in their PFM more so than they would with their personal medical doctor. Finding a PFM who meets both your personal and professional criteria may be an agonizing recruitment process, but it is of critical importance if your goal is to stay wealthy.

- **Private Financial Manager Requirements**

In high demand and short supply, the expert Private Financial Manager is aggressively sought after by the financially affluent. Not only because of their superior knowledge and ability, but also because they are committed to providing personalized services to a small number of important clients.

Lottery winners who wish to obtain these services will have to meet strict eligibility requirements. In general, the lottery winner will have to be a millionaire; but the best-of-the-best may only represent you if your net worth is at least $20 million.

- **Attorneys**

Lottery winners often begin their search for the PFM in the legal field. It is always good business to protect your legal environment first.

The lottery winner should only accept legal guidance from the individual who has received his/her Juris Doctorate (JD) from an accredited academic institution and is licensed to practice law in the state of your residence. The financially affluent often seek attorneys who are cross-trained in other professional areas.

Many licensed attorneys are also Certified Public Accountants (CPA). While the two distinctions are legally separated, this crossed-trained professional is often referred to as a "Tax Attorney" and is more likely to have the qualifications you need. One benefit of the Tax Attorney is that he/she is legally bound by the stringent attorney /client privilege, while at the same time holding a license to manage your tax affairs.

- **Certified Public Accountants (CPA)**

The minimum standard for the PFM should be that he/she is a licensed Certified Public Accountant (CPA). A licensed CPA has not only fulfilled the education and experience requirements in accordance with the State Boards of Accountancy, but he/she has also passed a rigorous national examination that certifies him/her as an accountant.

The CPA should be able to provide documentation that he/she has received continuing education in the ever-changing areas of tax law, estate planning and financial instruments. As a result of their professional growth, many CPAs will add a combination of professional titles, such as RIA, RR, ChFC or CFP to their designation.

- **Other Professional Qualifications**

If the PFM is an SEC *Registered Investment Advisor* (RIA), then you will know that he/she manages at least $25 million in *combined* investments and wealth. The PFM that manages less than $25 million is required to register with the security agency in their resident state of business. The Securities and Exchange Commission (SEC) keeps records of an

RIA's education, experience, fees and any disciplinary actions taken against them.

Meanwhile, the PFM who is a *Registered Representative* (RR) has passed an examination that meets the standards of the National Association of Securities Dealers (NASD). In general, this certification asserts that the individual has a good grasp of various investment vehicles and tools.

To hold the designation of *Chartered Financial Consultant* (ChFC), the PFM must have passed a series of ten courses ranging from retirement planning to taxation, estate planning to investments and from financial planning to insurance.

More popular though is the designation of *Certified Financial Planner* (CFP). Private Financial Managers with this certification have not only passed the same series of ten courses as the ChFC, but they have also passed an accumulative examination of the material learned. Furthermore, the CFP must have attained a minimum of three years of experience in financial counseling in order to receive this certification.

While all of these certifications, designations and tests enhance the professionals' skill set, none of them should be used exclusively in selecting the PFM. Lottery winners should also use the personal interview when recruiting a Private Financial Manager.

Sample Interview Questions

Meeting with and interviewing two or more of these true professionals is a critical step in finding the Private Financial Manager that is right for you. The following list of interview questions was designed to help the lottery winner focus on some of the most important professional criteria.

1. How long have you been an attorney, accountant and/or financial advisor and what firms or brokerages have you worked with?
2. What professional licenses do you hold?
3. How long and in what states have you been a licensed attorney and/or accountant?
4. Can you give me a description of your "typical" client and his/her wealth?
5. What continuing education courses have you taken in the past 5 years?
6. What are your professional strengths and how have you used them to benefit your clients?
7. On a scale from 1 to 10, with 1 being the least risky and 10 being the most risky, how would you rate your level of risk taking?
8. What types of investment tools or vehicles do you prefer to use?
9. Would you be willing to help me examine the information, reports or documents you bring me?
10. Can you provide me with some samples of your financial reports?
11. What is required of me, and do you mind explaining technical matters?
12. Would anyone besides you be allowed to access or make decisions about my financial portfolio?
13. Has any disciplinary action ever been taken against you by any professional organization?
14. Can you provide me with a few professional references?
15. How accessible would you be and would I have your home and cellular telephone numbers?

16. How would you protect my winnings from inflation, the IRS or loss?
17. How do your clients usually compensate you?
18. For the client with my wealth, what would you say is the average monthly fee that you charge?
19. Approximately how much time would you spend on my account- weekly and monthly?
20. As a Private Financial Manager, have you ever assisted clients in working with security consultants or the news media?

Paying the True Professional

Is it true that you get what you pay for? When it comes to professional advice and services, the answer is irrefutably ***yes***. Due to the seemingly large price tag for the services of true professionals, people who gain "windfall wealth" and who are unaccustomed to paying such premiums may consider the fees to be outrageous. However, when examined more closely it is obvious that premium fees paid for premium services are well worth the money.

This is not to say that you should agree to pay the PFM any amount they quote, but rather you should be open to compensating them for their talent, education, experience and dedication. At the same time, the lottery winner should avoid using the level of compensation as an exclusive criterion for recognizing the true professional.

Just because the junior professional typically earns a fee of approximately $100.00 per hour and the true professional may demand as much as $300.00 an hour, the price tag alone doesn't mean that he/she is necessarily right for you. You want to pay what is typical and ordinary for the services being rendered- neither more nor less than their other clients.

- **Types of Compensation**

It is important for the lottery winner to consider how the Private Financial Manager is compensated. There are two common ways in which professionals are paid: fee-based and commission-based compensation systems.

Most often, Private Financial Managers are paid by the professional hour, which is the arrangement of the fee-based compensation system. Under this structure, the client is billed for each hour (or part of an hour) spent working on his/her affairs. This method is so preferred that some professional organizations, such as the National Association of Personal Financial Advisors (NAPFA), require all licensees to be paid by the professional hour. It is widely held that the fee-based system facilitates more objective advice.

Meanwhile, others charge their clients under the commission-based compensation system. Under this system, payment for services is based on tasks as they are carried out, for making transactions, and/or for performance. It should not be ignored that investors who work for a percentage of what they make their client are likely to be more aggressive and risky with investments.

In fact, several large and recognizable firms were investigated in 2003 for fraudulent tax shelters they created to save the client money; and by extension earn higher commissions. Remember that most often it's not the financial advisor who is prosecuted for tax evasion, but rather the client who signs the legal forms.

So if you want to hold onto your lottery winnings, it is critical for you to find the true professional who is honest, trustworthy, educated, licensed, experienced, talented and who will always work in your best interest. This is the key to avoiding lotto-winner bankruptcy and enjoying your ticket to a life of luxury. – Good luck!

About the Author

Shayne Jones received his bachelor's degree in business administration (BBA) and his masters in public administration (MPA) from Georgia Southern University. He is continuing his post-graduate studies. With more than ten years of experience in the private sector and almost a decade in the public arena, Jones's work as a Coordinator on Georgia's Community Greenspace program (Senate Bill 399), created by former Governor Roy Barnes of Georgia, led him to the equally important task of analyzing policy as it relates to the benefits derived from lottery games.

In the State of Georgia alone, lottery players have sent over 550,000 four-year-olds to pre-kindergarten programs and given HOPE scholarships to over 725,000 students. Meanwhile, the Georgia Community Greenspace Program, which provides funds for counties to purchase land for informal recreation and natural resource protection, has safeguarded almost 500,000 (FY 2002) acres of land.[70] Governor Barnes' creation of such programs have provided protection for the environment as well as hope for tomorrow's generation.

A successful businessman and administrator, Shayne is a staunch supporter of state funded programs that encourage public participation and contribution. Since the origination of modern-day lotteries in New Hampshire, 1964, lottery ticket sales have provided states with resources to fund an abundance of environmental, social, health, rehabilitation, economic development and educational programs. If not for lotteries, even Harvard and Yale colleges would be without proper facilities.

By understanding the benefit created through playing lottery games and the winning process, it is Jones's belief that a higher player-participation rate can be achieved and an augmented social benefit can be enjoyed.

- Alan Gibson, *Managing Editor*

* Community Greenspace Program was created during the 2000 legislative session by enacting Senate Bill 399 (codified as *Official Code of Georgia Annotated* § 36-22-1 *et seq.*).

Acknowledgments

As any writer, I am indebted to the wonderful people who have helped me complete this project. From research to writing and editing, without their help and support this book would never have materialized.

I would like to give special thanks to the following: Pat Barnhart, *Executive Editor,* for her creative genius, insightful editing and formatting. Alan Gibson, *Managing Editor*, for his direction and editorial expertise. Susan Sowder, *Associate Editor,* for her thorough analysis and editing. Lin and Cheryl Shih of Stonepatch Design, for their art-to-market approach and cover design.

Equal thanks go out to the lottery winners who generously participated in interviews, and the media sources and non-profit organizations that were gracious with their material. Another debt of gratitude goes to the personnel in the various federal, state and lottery agency offices across the United States who gave way to the freedom of information. For without their assistance, the policy, data, trends, and processes that lend this book its credibility would be forgone.

Finally, I would like to extend a heartfelt personal thanks to my family for their unyielding support and encouragement throughout this assignment. My parents especially were an objective sounding board and source of wisdom for many aspects of this work. Thank you one and all!

\- Shayne Jones

Notes

1. National Council on Problem Gambling. Inc. June 1, 2004 www.ncpgambling.org
2. Ibid
3. Gamblers Anonymous, Los Angeles, CA, June 1, 2004 www.gamblersanonymous.org
4. ©2004*Atlanta Journal-Constitution*, June 29, 2003. Reprinted with permission from the A.J.C.
5. North America Association of State and Provincial Lotteries (NASPL), April, 2004, www.naspl.org
6. National Weather Service, Silver Spring, MD, March, 2004 www.lightningsafety.noaa.gov
7. Ibid
8. North America Association of State and Provincial Lotteries (NASPL), April, 2004, www.naspl.org
9. *Marietta Daily Journal*, "Marietta Lotto Winners enjoying lives of luxury", 7/26/2003, Phillip Giltman
10. Texas Lottery Commission, January 2001, www.txlottery.org/info/reports.cfm
11. Minnesota State Lottery, and Saint Cloud University, February 2004 www.lottery.state.mn.us/gambling.html
12. Texas Lottery Commission, January 2001 www.txlottery/info/reports.cfm
13. Minnesota State Lottery, and Saint Cloud University, February 2004 Survey, www.lottery.state.mn.us/gambling.html
14. Texas Lottery Commission, January 2001 www.txlottery/info/reports.cfm
15. U.S. Census Bureau, Annual Estimates of the Population for the United States and Puerto Rico: April 1, 2000 to July 1, 2004 http://census.gov/popest/states/tables/NST-EST2004-01.pdf
16. Ibid
17. The Gallup Organization, Gambling a Common Activity for Americans, Growth in casino gambling, 3-24-04, Jeffrey M. Jones
18. Texas Lottery Commission, January 2001, www.txlottery.org/info/reports.cfm
19. Minnesota State Lottery, and Saint Cloud University, February 2004 www.lottery.state.mn.us/gambling.html
20. Ibid
21. Ibid
22. Ibid
23. Ibid

24. Texas Lottery Commission, January 2001 www.txlottery/info/reports.cfm
25. Minnesota State Lottery, and Saint Cloud University, February 2004 Survey, www.lottery.state.mn.us/gambling.html
26. Tennessee Code Unannotated §4-51-115, Lottery Retailers, Chapter 51, Part 1, General Provisions
27. United States Code, Title 18 Crimes and Criminal Procedures, Part 1- Crimes, Chapter 61- LOTTERIES, Section 1301. Importing and Transporting Lottery Tickets. January 6, 2003
28. United States Code, Title 18 Crimes and Criminal Procedures, Part 1- Crimes, Chapter 61- LOTTERIES, Section 1302. Importing and Transporting Lottery Tickets. January 6, 2003
29. *Marietta Daily Journal*, "Marietta Lotto Winners enjoying lives of luxury", 7/26/2003, Phillip Giltman
30. Ibid
31. © Multi-State Lottery Association (MUSL), *Powerball, It's America's Game, Jerry Berggren & Cathy DeMuynck*, March 27, 2002, www.musl.com/0327021a.shtm
32. Ibid
33. Ibid
34. Ibid
35. ©2004*Atlanta Journal-Constitution*, June 29, 2003. Reprinted with permission from the A.J.C.
36. Ibid
37. Ibid
38. Ibid
39. *Louisville Courier-Journal*, "Powerball win is dream come true for Hoosiers", March 16, 2004, by Joe Follick and Lesley Stedman Weidenbener
40. ©2004*Atlanta Journal-Constitution (A.J.C.)* June 29, 2003. Reprinted with permission from the A.J.C.
41. ©Multi-State Lottery Association (MUSL), *Powerball, It's America's Game, James and Sharon Lewis,* August 16, 2000
42. National Safety Council, 2001 Report, Odds of Death due to Injury
43. Ibid
44. *Marietta Daily Journal*, "Marietta Lotto Winners enjoying lives of luxury", 7 /26/2003, Phillip Giltman
45. ©2004*Atlanta Journal-Constitution*, June 29, 2003. Reprinted with permission from the A.J.C.
46. Ibid
47. Ibid
48. Central Intelligence Agency, World Fact Book, 2003

49. Internal Revenue Service, Department of the Treasury, 2004
50. Ibid
51. Divorce Headquarters, *Missed Day in Court Leads to $880,000 Child Support Order*, August 9, 2000
52. Office of Child Support Enforcement, 2004, www.acf.dhhs.gov/programs/cse
53. *Louisville Courier-Journal*, "Powerball win is dream come true for Hoosiers", March 16, 2004, by Joe Follick and Lesley Stedman Weidenbener
54. ©2004*Atlanta Journal-Constitution*, June 29, 2003. Reprinted with permission from the A.J.C.
55. ©Multi-State Lottery Association (MUSL), *Powerball, It's America's Game, James and Sharon Lewis,* August 16, 2000
56. U.S. Census Bureau, www.census/gov/population /www/socdemo/marr-div.html
57. CDC, National Center for Health Statistics, 2003-Marriage and Divorce, www.cdc.gov/nchs/fastats/divorce.htm
58. Wisconsin State Journal, 5/22/1998, Lottery Winner Gets Jail For Perjury- Man Tried To Hide Winnings During Divorce.
59. In re Marriage of DENISE and THOMAS ROSSI, 90 Cal. App.4th (Cal. App. 2nd District 2001) (Case Number B141041) (Super Ct. No. BD250668)
60. CDC, National Center for Health Statistics, New Report Sheds Light on Trends and Patterns in Marriage, Divorce, and Cohabitation. www.cdc.gov/nchs/pressroom/02news/div_mar_cohab.htm
61. Alston v. Alston, 629 A. 2d 70 (Md. 1993)
62. Ibid
63. Associated Press, *Pop culture watchers say technology helps create generation of attention seekers*. By Martha Irvine www.ap.org, ©Reprinted with permission of the Associated Press
64. Ibid
65. U.S. Department of Justice, U.S. Attorney's Office of the Southern District of Texas, June 4, 2003, Press Release
66. © Multi-State Lottery Association (MUSL), *Powerball, It's America's Game, James and Sharon Lewis,* August 16, 2000
67. Ibid
68. *Marietta Daily Journal*, "Marietta Lotto Winners enjoying lives of luxury",7/26/2003, Phillip Giltman
69. © Multi-State Lottery Association (MUSL), *Powerball, It's America's Game, James and Sharon Lewis,* August 16, 2000
70. Georgia Department of Natural Resources, January 31, 2004